REVISED

C'EST À TOI!

Level One

Workbook

Sharon Norlander
Sarah Vaillancourt
Christine Gensmer

EMC/Paradigm Publishing, Saint Paul, Minnesota

Editorial Development: Course Crafters, Inc.
Newburyport, MA

Illustrations: Renegade Studios
P. J. Gruen
C. C. King
Grace Meyer

Design and Production: All Night Illustration
Susan Bond

ISBN 0-8219-2265-3

Published by EMC/Paradigm Publishing
875 Montreal Way
St. Paul, Minnesota 55102
800-328-1452
http://www.emcp.com
E-mail: educate@emcp.com

Printed in the United States of America
21 XXX 14

CONTENTS

Unité 1   *Salut! Ça va?*

1 | Fill in each empty speech bubble with one of the following sentences.

Allô, Jacques?

Je m'appelle André.

Je te présente Marc.

Pardon?

Bonjour, Marie!

3. _____

1. _____

4. _____

2. _____

5. _____

C'EST À TOI!
Level One

2 Write the appropriate greeting to say hello to each of the following people.

Modèle:

Bonjour, Mademoiselle.

1. _____

3. _____

2. _____

4. _____

3 Élisabeth and Fabrice Dupont are expecting a baby. They live in the United States but want to give their child a French name. They found the lists of names on page 3 in a baby book and have asked for your help. Choose the names you like best, listing seven possible names for a daughter and seven possible names for a son. (The lists include popular names, names from the Middle Ages, names from one century ago, literary names, regional names, names derived from flowers and hyphenated names.)

Names for a Daughter	**Names for a Son**
1. _____	1. _____
2. _____	2. _____
3. _____	3. _____
4. _____	4. _____
5. _____	5. _____
6. _____	6. _____
7. _____	7. _____

Les prénoms les plus souvent donnés

Caroline	Julien	Sophie
Céline	Laurent	Stéphane
Christophe	Nathalie	Stéphanie
Corinne	Nicolas	Thomas
Isabelle	Sandrine	Virginie
Julie	Sébastien	

Des prénoms du Moyen Âge

Amaury	Guenièvre	Nicolette
Éléonore	Lancelot	Thibaut

Des prénoms d'il y a 100 ans

Bérengère	Émilie	Justine
Camille	Gaëtan	Léonard
Clémence	Gaston	Mélanie
Delphine	Gladys	

Des prénoms littéraires

Anaïs	Clément	Hugo
Andréa	Damian	Rebecca
Aurélie	Emma	

Des prénoms régionaux

Gaëlle	Gwenaël	Kevin

Des prénoms de fleurs

Anne-Fleur	Églantine	Fleur-Amanda
Capucine		

Marie et Jean, donnés en composé

Marie-Alice	Marie-Anna	Jean-Philippe
Marie-André	Jean-Noël	Jean-Baptiste
Marie-France	Jean-Marc	Jean-Michel
Marie-Julie		

4 | **A.**   Here are some birth announcements from a French newspaper. For each announcement fill in the chart on page 5. The first one has been done for you.

naissances

M. Lucien ALLIOLI
et Mme, née
Stéphanie Lefèvre,
ont la joie de vous annoncer
la naissance d'
Aymeric
Paris, le 7 juin 2002.

M. Michel BONNET
et Mme, née
Géraldine Leblanc,
laissent à Guillaume,
Charles-Édouard et Amaury
la joie d'annoncer
la naissance d'
Astrid
Paris, le 4 juin 2002.

Bertrand et Svetlana
DODILLE
ont la joie d'annoncer
la naissance de leur fils
Sacha
Bucarest, le 14 juin 2002.

M. Rémi ESCLATTIER
et Mme, née Caroline Batard,
partagent avec Aliénor
et Pétronille le plaisir
d'annoncer la naissance de
Théophanie
Neuilly-sur-Seine,
le 9 juin 2002.

M. Armand
GÉRARD-TASSET
et Mme, née
Geneviève Jeannin,
et Sixtine
ont la joie d'annoncer
la naissance d'
Axel
Angoulême, le 31 mai 2002.

M. Vincent GRENET
et Mme, née Marie-France
Pagezy,
partagent avec David
la joie de vous annoncer
la naissance de
Luc
Paris, le 1er juin 2002.

M. Pascal
HERMENT
et Mme, née Jacqueline Corbin,
ont la joie d'annoncer
la naissance de
Sébastien
Paris, le 11 juin 2002.

Le docteur Gérard
DELLON
et Mme, née
Patrice Merle,
Mathilde et Laurent
ont la joie d'annoncer
la naissance de
Yolaine
Versailles, le 4 juin 2002.

M. Gérard
BOIS
et Mme, née
Christiane Moreau,
partagent avec Caroline
le plaisir d'annoncer
la naissance de
Roman
Champigny, le 5 juin 2002.

M. François
MARTIN
et Mme, née
Nathalie Toussaint,
ont la joie de vous annoncer
la naissance de
Sophie
St.-Maur, le 30 mai 2002.

Name of Child	Date of Birth	City of Birth	Father's First Name	Mother's First Name	Family Name
Aymeric	June 7, 2002	Paris	Lucien	Stéphanie	ALLIOLI

B.   Notice how the family's last name is printed in each announcement on page 4. Complete this sentence: In French, last names usually are written in _____ letters.

C.   Notice how dates are written in the announcements. Answer the following questions.

1.   In French dates, what is written first: the month, the day or the year?

_____

2.   What is written second?

_____

3.   What is written last?

_____

D.   Of the following list of French names, which would you choose as your own? Why? Using your new name, introduce yourself in French.

Prénoms de filles	Prénoms de garçons
Adja	Abdoul
Angèle	Benoît
Brigitte	Christian
Cécile	Claude
Émilie	Didier
Gabrielle	François
Irène	Frédéric
Josiane	Grégoire
Lisette	Jacques
Magali	Laurent
Nicole	Malick
Renée	Pascal
Simone	Raymond
Virginie	Salim
Zakia	Victor

_____

_____

_____

_____

_____

_____

5 | Complete the following crossword puzzle by writing the indicated numbers in French.

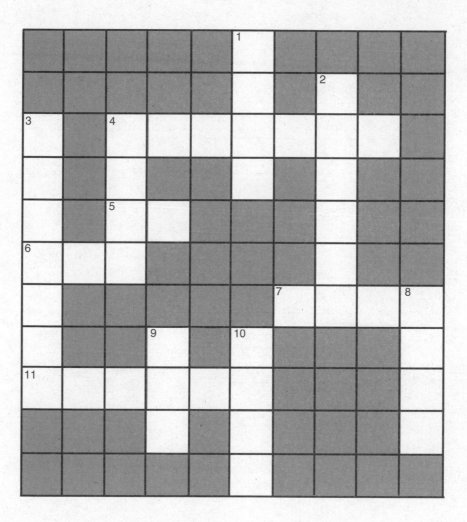

Horizontalement		Verticalement	
4.	19	1.	5
5.	1	2.	4
6.	6	3.	17
7.	0	4.	2
11.	13	8.	11
		9.	10
		10.	7

C'EST À TOI!
Level One

6 | Write out the following numbers in French.

1. 8 _____

2. 3 _____

3. 12 _____

4. 14 _____

5. 9 _____

6. 18 _____

7. 16 _____

8. 15 _____

9. 20 _____

10. 0 _____

11. 7 _____

12. 10 _____

13. 2 _____

14. 11 _____

15. 5 _____

16. 1 _____

17. 19 _____

18. 4 _____

19. 6 _____

20. 13 _____

7 You can hear only what Marie is saying on the phone. Imagine what her friend Karine is saying on the other end and fill in the empty speech bubbles.

1.

3.

2.

4.

8 | A. Look at the following advertisements. For each one decide if it is from Paris, Saint-Malo or Nice. Then write the corresponding phone number in the appropriate column in the chart on page 11.

Paris	Saint-Malo	Nice

B. Complete the following missing information using the advertisements on page 10.

You already know that phone numbers in Paris begin with 01. Phone numbers in Saint-Malo begin with _____ , and phone numbers in Nice begin with _____ .

9 There has been a cross-cultural misunderstanding in each of the following situations. Read each passage and then choose the best reason for the misunderstanding. Base your choice only on the specific information given in the passage and your comprehension of the cultural information presented in this unit.

Modèle: Kim was surprised on the first day of school when her French teacher greeted Fez, a foreign exchange student, by asking him if he missed the climate in Morocco. Why did Kim's teacher assume that Fez was from Morocco?

     A. The teacher had already met Fez.

     B. In French-speaking Africa, surnames vary from country to country.

     C. In French-speaking Africa, children may be named after a city, such as Fez, Morocco.

The correct answer is **C**. *A is incorrect because you have no way of knowing whether or not the teacher had already met Fez.* **B** *is incorrect because Fez is a first name, not a surname. In French-speaking Africa, children may be named after a city. Therefore,* **C** *is the best answer.*

1. Brad was staying with the Villette family in Amiens, France. One day while Madame Villette was busy, Brad answered the phone for her, saying **Bonjour**. Why did Madame Villette later correct Brad?

     A. Brad shouldn't have picked up the phone.

     B. Brad should have said **Allô**.

     C. Brad should have let the phone ring a few more times before he answered it.

2. While staying with a French family in Rennes, Charles, an American exchange student, was startled during dinner one evening when Monsieur Joyaux referred to him as **le roi** (*the king*). Why did Monsieur Joyaux call Charles **le roi**?

    A. Monsieur Joyaux was making reference to the fact that first names in France may refer to former French royalty.

    B. Charles was being a snob.

    C. In France **le roi** is a common nickname.

3. While looking up the phone number of Jacques Rambert, a friend in Paris, Sam was surprised when he came across the names Mohamed Ramadan, Stéfano Ramazzoti, José Ramos and Wendy Ramsay. Why were these names in the Paris phone book?

    A. They are all traditional French names.

    B. French phone books include the names and phone numbers of important people who live in other countries.

    C. Today, names reflect the multicultural makeup of French society.

4. While staying with a family in Quebec, Becky found it exasperating when she tried to talk to the host student at a family reunion. The student, his father and his grandfather would all look at her when she said "Robert" because they all had the same name. Why were all three people named Robert?

    A. French-Canadian families often pass along first names.

    B. The family wanted a name that was spelled the same in both French and English.

    C. Canadian law requires parents to name their firstborn son Robert.

Unité 2 *Qu'est-ce que tu aimes faire?*

Leçon A

1 | **A.** Draw a line from each expression to its corresponding picture.

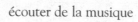

jouer au foot

écouter de la musique

skier

téléphoner

regarder la télé

nager

étudier

jouer au basket

C'EST À TOI!
Level One

B. How would you answer the question **Qu'est-ce que tu aimes faire**? Choose three expressions from the previous activity to complete the following sentences.

1. J'aime _____

2. J'aime _____

3. J'aime _____

2 | A **centre de loisirs** provides French people with the opportunity to participate in many activities, including sports. Look at the description of the **Plage de Villennes**, a popular **centre de loisirs** located just outside Paris, and then answer the questions that follow.

> **Centre de loisirs**
>
> **PLAGE DE VILLENNES.** 27 km de Paris, Autoroute A13, sortie Poissy Villennes. Rens: 02.39.75.82.03 et 02.39.75.82.83. Dans une île, traversée de la Seine permanente par bateau. Piscines, Tennis (terre battue), ping pong, golfs miniatures, volley, basket, jeux de plein air, ski nautique, solarium naturiste, sauna, restaurant, pizzeria, crêperie, aires de pique-nique, aires de jeux, toboggan nautique géant 75 m. Possibilité de croisière sur la Seine. Ouvert tlj de 10h à 19h, dim jusqu'à 19h30. Tarifs semaine: Adulte 7,01€, enf. (4 à 12 ans) 4,75€. Tarifs samedi, dimanche et jrs fériés: Adulte 8,69€, enf. 5,79€. Parking ombragé gratuit. Chenils gratuits. Jusqu'au 30 septembre.

1. In which of the following activities can people participate at the **Plage de Villennes**? Circle your choices.

   jouer au foot   jouer au basket   jouer au volley

   regarder la télé   écouter de la musique

   aller au cinéma   jouer au tennis

2. What are two other activities offered at the **Plage de Villennes**?

   _____

   _____

3. What two phone numbers could you call to get more information about the **Plage de Villennes**?

   _____

   _____

4. What words indicate that they serve food at the **Plage de Villennes**?

   _____

3 | Complete each speech bubble with one of the following subject pronouns.

J'   Tu   Il   Elle   Nous   Vous   Ils   Elles

Modèle:

Tu aimes regarder la télé?

3. _____ aime skier.

6. _____ aiment jouer au foot.

1. _____ aimez écouter de la musique?

4. _____ aime téléphoner.

7. _____ aiment étudier.

2. _____ aimes jouer au basket?

5. _____ aimez nager, Madame?

8. _____ aiment aller au cinéma.

C'EST À TOI!
Level One

4 Christopher is anxiously awaiting the arrival of Georges, a French exchange student who will be staying at his home. He wrote a letter to Georges asking about things he likes to do in his free time. Georges faxed the following response to Christopher. Circle the present tense verb forms and underline the infinitives.

FAX

DATE: 10/3
TO: Christopher
FROM: Georges

MESSAGE:
Salut, Christopher!
J'(arrive) demain. J'aime <u>aller</u> au cinéma. Je joue au foot et je nage. Tu aimes jouer au foot? J'aime écouter de la musique et regarder la télé.

À bientôt!
Georges

---

5 Write six logical sentences, each using a subject pronoun from Column A, the appropriate form of one of the verbs from Column B and an expression from Column C.

A	B	C
1. je	aimer	la télé
2. tu	étudier	au basket
3. il	jouer	bien
4. nous	écouter	au foot
5. vous	regarder	de la musique
6. elles	nager	pour l'interro

1. _____
2. _____
3. _____
4. _____
5. _____
6. _____

6 | Complete each sentence by telling what various people are doing, according to the illustrations.

Modèle:

Delphine *nage.* _____

4. Nous _____

1. M. Dupuis _____

5. Tu _____

2. Karine et Marc _____

6. Vous _____

3. Je _____

7. Luc et Raphaël _____

Leçon B

7 | Draw a line from each question to the best answer.

1. Luc aime faire du sport?
2. Tu aimes le camping?
3. Cécile écoute de la musique?
4. Vous aimez regarder la télé?
5. Vous aimez jouer au basket?

a. Oui, j'aime les films.
b. Oui, il aime faire du roller.
c. Oui, nous aimons beaucoup jouer au basket.
d. Oui, j'aime bien le camping.
e. Oui, elle aime le rock.

8 | Use the following list of youth-oriented community education classes to answer the questions on page 19.

ARTS ET ÉDUCATION

Arr.	Centre	Stages proposés:
15e	**Brancion** 18, avenue de la Porte-de-Brancion ☎ 01 48 42 32 25	• **Modern jazz:** du 7 au 13 juillet — 10–15 ans — 22,87€ • **Informatique:** du 7 au 13 juillet — 10–15 ans — 22,87€ • **Photo:** du 7 au 13 juillet — 11–15 ans — 22,87€ • **Vidéo:** du 7 au 13 juillet — 13–16 ans — 22,87€
16e	**Le Point-du-Jour** 1, rue du Général- Malleterre ☎ 01 45 25 14 19	Stages de 5 jours: • **Tennis:** juillet, août, septembre — 129,58€/stage • **Jazz:** en juillet — 60,98€/stage • **Guitare:** juillet et août — 50,31€/stage • **Peinture:** juillet et août — 68,60€/stage • **Poterie:** septembre — 68,60€/stage • **Céramique (raku):** 1re semaine de juillet — 99,09€/stage
18e	**La Chapelle** 32, boulevard de la Chapelle ☎ 01 42 05 18 39	• **Peinture — arts plastiques:** du 12 au 30 juillet — 12–13 ans — gratuit
	Hébert 12, rue des Fillettes ☎ 01 42 09 09 98	• **Piscine, tennis, basket, football, bowling:** du 4 au 30 juillet
19e	**Jules-Romains** 17, rue Jules-Romains ☎ 01 42 39 68 54	• **Karting:** stage en projet • **Vidéo multimédia:** une semaine — 45,73€ • **Multi-activités:** à la semaine 10–18 h — piscine, bowling, pique-nique — 30,49€/semaine
	Clavel 26, rue Clavel ☎ 01 42 40 87 78	• **Sculpture:** du 4 au 8 juillet
	Curial 90, rue Curial ☎ 01 40 35 56 59	• **Stages en projet:** contacter le centre
	Mathis 11, rue Mathis ☎ 01 40 34 50 80	• **Théâtre vidéo reportage, improvisation:** 18 ans — 53,36€/semaine • **Informatique-graphisme réalisation de maquettes, affiches et** **journal:** adolescents — 53,36€/semaine • **Karaté initiation:** 53,36€/semaine • **Cirque initiation:** 53,36€/semaine

1. In which city are the community centers located? (HINT: Look at their phone numbers.)

    _____

2. At which community center can you take a soccer class?

    _____

3. If you like sports, at which community center can you get the widest selection of interesting classes?

    _____

4. At which two community centers can you take a music class? What type of music do they offer?

    _____

    _____

5. If you want to take a class on making movies, would it be less expensive to go to Brancion or Jules-Romains?

    _____

    _____

6. Which five classes offered at these community centers appeal to you the most?

    _____

    _____

9 | For each of the illustrations on page 20, fill in the face to show how much you like the indicated activity. Then write a sentence that tells how much you like it.

un peu

bien

beaucoup

Modèle:

3.

6.

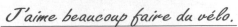

J'aime beaucoup faire du vélo.

1.

4.

7.

2.

5.

1. _____
2. _____
3. _____
4. _____
5. _____
6. _____
7. _____

10 | **A.** Here is a list of some types of music that are popular in France. Tell where each one originated.

1. la cold

   _____

2. la musique créole

   _____

3. le world beat

   _____

4. le rap

   _____

B. Answer the questions that follow about music trends in France. Then use your answers to write a composition in English comparing popular music in France with popular music where you live. Begin your composition with an introduction that explains what you will be comparing. Finish your composition with a conclusion that summarizes your comparisons.

1. What are popular subjects for the lyrics of contemporary French songs?

2. What types of music do French teens like?

3. Do French teens like only songs with French lyrics?

   _____

   _____

   _____

   _____

   _____

   _____

   _____

   _____

   _____

   _____

   _____

   _____

Leçon C

11 Use the illustrations to help you fill in the blanks in the puzzle with the names of the related sports activities. The answers may be either nouns or verbs.

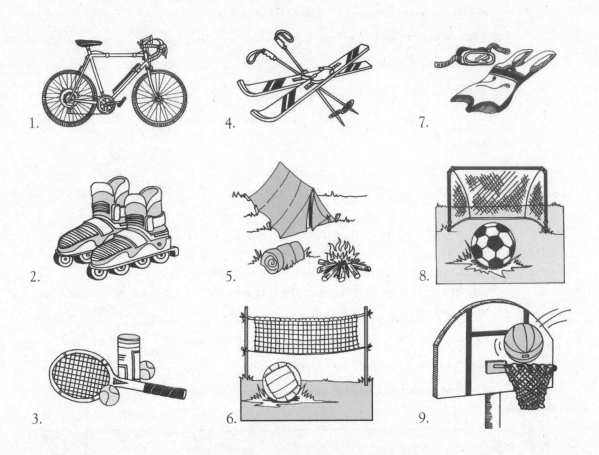

1.   4.   7.

2.   5.   8.

3.   6.   9.

L E S   S P O R T S

12 Look at the activities that follow and decide where they are normally done. Then, list those that are usually done indoors in the circle on the left and those that are usually done outdoors in the circle on the right. Where the two circles intersect, list those activities that can be done either indoors or outdoors.

manger de la pizza	nager	faire du footing
jouer au tennis	étudier	téléphoner
dormir	jouer au basket	écouter de la musique
jouer aux jeux vidéo	jouer au volley	skier
faire du roller	danser	jouer au foot
faire du vélo	faire les devoirs	
regarder la télé	lire	

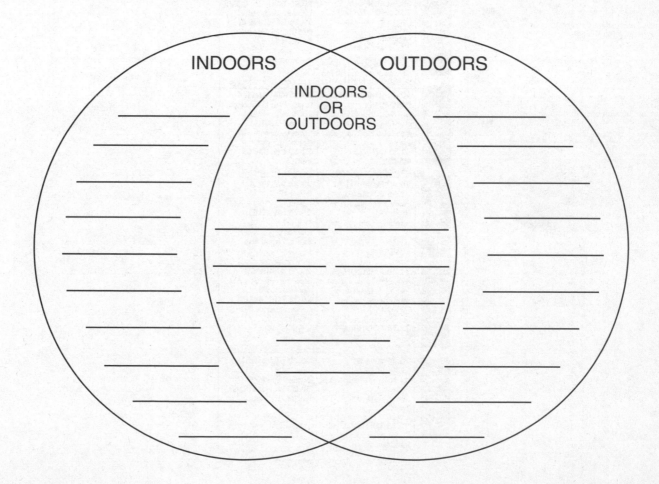

C'EST À TOI!
Level One

13 | Look at the following television schedule and circle the sports programs.

TF1

a2

SAMEDI

20.40 MONDIAL 97
20.55 FOOTBALL
Coupe du monde en direct de Rome: Italie/Autriche.
22.55 USHUAIA
Le magazine de l'extrême proposé par Nicolas Hulot et Geneviève Bruno.

20.35 CHAMPS-ÉLYSÉES
Spécial Nîmes.
22.50 TENNIS ROLAND-GARROS
Les meilleurs morceaux choisis.
23.40 CONCERT S.O.S. RACISME
Paris-Prague-Moscou.

DIMANCHE

20.40 MONDIAL 97
20.55 FOOTBALL
Coupe du monde en direct de Milan: R.F.A./Belgique.
22.55 SPÉCIAL SPORTS
Grand Prix de Formule 1 du Canada en différé de Montréal.

20.30 MAIGRET À NEW YORK
Téléfilm de Stéphane Bertin, avec Jean Richard, R. Pellegrin.
22.15 TENNIS ROLAND-GARROS
Les morceaux choisis.
23.15 FOOTBALL
Coupe du monde: Brésil/Suède.

LUNDI

20.40 MONDIAL 97
20.55 FOOTBALL
Coupe du monde en direct de Cagliari: Angleterre/Eire.
22.55 CHOCS
Émission proposée par Claude Maggiori. Ce soir: Rétrospective des meilleures séquences de l'émission.

20.40 COUP DE CŒUR
Émission de variétés.
22.15 DESSEINS ET DESTIN DE CHARLES DE GAULLE
Documentaire.
La rencontre (1).

MARDI

20.40 UNE AFFAIRE D'HOMMES
Film de Nicolas Ribowski, avec Claude Brasseur, Jean-Louis Trintignant, Jean Carmet.
22.35 CIEL MON MARDI!
Émission de Christophe

20.35 ANTIPASTI
Le journal de la Coupe du monde de football.
20.56 FOOTBALL
Coupe du monde: Hollande/Égypte.
22.50 L'HEURE DE VÉRITÉ
Invité: Édouard Balladur.

MERCREDI

20.40 MONDIAL 97
20.55 FOOTBALL
Coupe du monde en direct de Naples: Argentine/Colombie.

20.30 PARTIR À DEUX
Téléfilm.
22.25 MY TÉLÉ IS RICH
Émission proposée par Patrick Poivre d'Arvor.

JEUDI

20.40 PAPAROFF
Paparoff se dédouble. Téléfilm de Denys de la Patellière, avec Michel Constantin, Michel Duchaussoy, Pascale Petit.
22.15 FOOTBALL
Coupe du monde: Cameroun/Autriche.

20.40 ANTIPASTI
Le journal de la Coupe du monde de football.
20.56 FOOTBALL
Coupe du monde: Italie/États-Unis.

VENDREDI

20.40 AVIS DE RECHERCHE
Les meilleurs moments de la Une.
Avec J.-P. Foucault, P. Sébastien, J. Hallyday, Eros Ramzzotti, Vanessa Paradis.
22.35 FOOTBALL
Coupe du monde: R.F.A./Émirats.

20.40 L'AMI GIONO
Série.
Les déserteurs (6/6).
23.35 LA PUNITION
Film de Jean Rouch.

14 | Write complete sentences using the indicated expressions. Use the appropriate present tense form of each verb.

Modèle: je / ne… pas / jouer au tennis

    Je ne joue pas au tennis.

1. je / ne… pas / jouer au basket

_____

2. tu / ne… pas / danser bien

_____

3. vous / ne… pas / nager beaucoup

_____

4. nous / ne… pas / jouer au tennis

_____

5. il / ne… pas / étudier pour l'interro

_____

6. elles / ne… pas / aimer le rock

_____

15 | Determine the context of the reading below and of those on pages 26–28 by telling what each is and who would read it.

1. What is this?

_____

Who would read it?

_____

Salades Composées

Salade Niçoise .... 6,40€
Salade, thon, olives, œuf dur, anchois, poivron, tomates

Salade 4 Saisons .... 5,03€
Crudités de saison

Salade Saint-Michel .... 5,79€
Salade, jambon épaule, gruyère, pomme

Salade Mixte .... 4,57€
Salade, tomates, œuf dur

Salade de Poulet .... 6,40€
Salade, poulet, gruyère, mayonnaise

Salade Campagnarde .... 6,40€
Salade, pommes de terre à l'huile, Cantal, jambon cru

PAIN POILÂNE

TARTINE : Pâté ou Rillettes
ou Saucisson sec .... 3,51€
Bleu d'Auvergne .... 4,12€
Jambon Cru .... 5,03€
Croque Campagnard .... 5,03€

Sandwiches

Rillettes paysannes .... 2,29€   Fromage .... 2,29€

Pâté de campagne .... 2,29€   Mixte (jambon et gruyère) .... 4,42€

Jambon de Paris .... 2,29€   Club Sandwich .... 5,95€
Poulet, tomate, œuf dur, salade, mayonnaise

Jambon de pays .... 4,42€   Saucisses chaudes .... 3,66€

Saucisson d'Auvergne .... 2,29€   Hot-Dog .... 4,42€

Le Végétarien .... 4,42€   Pain Poilâne supplément .... 0,76€
Salade, tomate, œuf dur, mayonnaise

2. What is this?

_____

Who would read it?

_____

• TENNIS

**ASSOCIATION SPORTIVE
DE ROTHENEUF,**
75-77, av. du Cdt-L'Herminier, **St-Malo**
Tél. : 02 99 40 54 89.
STADE DE LA JACQUES-CARTIER,
Avenue de la Borderie, **St-Malo**
Tél. : 02 99 56 45 68.
STADE DUGUAY-TROUIN,
Paramé **St-Malo.**
Tél. : 02 99 40 31 40.
TENNIS-CLUB DE LA J.A.,
19, bd Gouazon.
Tél. : 02 99 81 23 62.
TENNIS MUNICIPAUX,
- Parc des Sports de Marville,
  St-Malo.
- Salle de Rocabey.
  Tél. : 02 99 56 41 04.
- Salle du Naye.

3. What is this?

_____

Who would read it?

_____

COOKIES

POUR 4 PERSONNES   **DIVERS**

PRÉPARATION
10 minutes

CUISSON
25 minutes

SOMMELIER
Menthe fraîche ou thé chaud

ÉLÉMENTS DE BASE
- 75 g de beurre
- 1 œuf
- 75 g de sucre de canne
- quelques gouttes de vanille liquide
- 150 g de farine
- 1 cuillerée à café de levure chimique
- 1/2 cuillerée à café de sel
- 100 g de chocolat noir

Faire ramollir le beurre à température ambiante. Y incorporer le sucre de canne, ajouter l'œuf entier, l'essence de vanille et mélanger le tout intimement.

Ajouter ensuite petit à petit la farine et la levure en tournant sans cesse avec une spatule, saler et ajouter enfin le chocolat préalablement coupé en très petits dés. Beurrer une plaque allant au four. À l'aide d'une cuillère à soupe, former les cookies sur la plaque, puis les faire cuire à four chaud (thermostat 7) pendant 10 à 15 minutes. Les cookies se dégustent froids ou encore tièdes.

4. What is this?

_____

Who would read it?

_____

Garage Mécanique

Mannespièces Ivry rech.
Réceptionnaire
MÉCANICIENS
P2 - P3
Tél. 01.46.72.36.36

Sté dépannages rech. Dépanneur pouvant assurer une permanence 1 w.-end sur 2. Étudie ttes propos.
Tél. 02.39.47.06.00

CONCESSIONNAIRE
PEUGEOT
Les Ulis
recrute
2 VENDEURS
QUALIFIÉS
SECTEUR
1 jne Vendeur
SECTEUR

1 VENDEUR
Magasin VN VO

1 VENDEUSE
Magasin VN VO

1 SECRÉTAIRE
COMMERCIALE

FORMATION ASSURÉE

Env. CV + lettre + photo à l'attent. du Chef des vtes
12 rue de la Réunion
Z.A. de COURTABŒUF
91940 LES ULIS

FORD
ROCHEBRUNE
recherche
MAGASINIER
PIÈCES DÉTACHÉES
Connaissance de la marque souhaitée.
Tél. pr RV à Philippe
LE GRALL 01 48 05 29 02

Hôtellerie Restauration

IHR RECRUTE
6 ÉTAGÈRES
5 COMMIS DE CUISINE
5 CHEFS DE PARTIE
ETT 01 40 44 68 89

WORKFORCE ETT
CUISINIERS
ÉTAGÈRES
Se prés. av. réf. dès 7h
ETT 54 r. N.D. de Lorette
PARIS 9e 01.40.16.16.13

Recherche Serveurs et Commis de cuisine pour Restaurant Asnières
(92) Tél. 01 40 86 98 92

Recherche urgent
PIZZAIOLO
Tél. 01.48.95.27.63

La qualification du personnel est notre préoccupation. Vous avez entre 17 et 23 ans, Homme ou Femme. Le Groupe de Restauration

GÉRARD JOULIE
vous offre dans le cadre d'un contrat qualification d'une durée de 12 mois, une formation rémunérée pour les métiers de :
CUISINIER
ET DE
CHEF DE RANG
Venez rejoindre notre UNITÉ ÉCOLE en vous présentant ce jour et demain avec CV au Restaurant BATIFOL
154 r. St Charles
75015 Paris Me Lourmel
Tél. 01.45.54.52.09
SIÈGE SOCIAL
Philippe BROSSIER
Tél. 01.49.84.67.67

RESTAURANTS ET SITES
ACCOR
CAFÉTÉRIA DU MUSÉE
LE LOUVRE
75058 Paris cédex 01
recherche
EMPLOYÉ (E) de cafétéria temps partiel (serv. midi)
Se prés. ce jour de 16h à 18h à la Cafétéria Publique
Me Palais Royal

5. What is this?

_____

Who would read it?

_____

MESSAGE

Communication reçue à_____ heures, le_____

de M _____

pour M _____

☐ a téléphoné sans laisser de message,

☐ demande de le rappeler au N°_____

☐ a laissé le message suivant: _____

_____ Sophie de Guibert _____

16/73 92 50 51

_____

_____

_____

6. What is this?

_____

Who would read it?

_____

Unité 3 *Au café*

1 How would each of the following people answer the question **Comment vas-tu?**

1. _____

3. _____

2. _____

4. _____

2 | Fill in the speech bubbles to complete the conversation according to the description of each illustration.

1. Malika and Marie-France greet each other.

2. Malika asks Marie-France how she is and Marie-France says she is thirsty.

3. Marie-France invites Malika to go to the café.

4. Malika is hungry and prefers to go to a fast-food restaurant.

5. Marie-France agrees to go to the fast-food restaurant.

3 | Draw a line from each question in Column A to its most logical answer in Column B.

A		B	
1.	On va au cinéma?	a.	Non, je joue bien au volley.
2.	Quelle heure est-il?	b.	Non, j'étudie pour l'interro.
3.	Tu aimes les fast-foods?	c.	Il est quatre heures.
4.	Comment vas-tu?	d.	J'aime faire du vélo.
5.	Tu t'appelles comment?	e.	J'ai soif.
6.	Qu'est-ce que tu aimes faire?	f.	Je m'appelle Sophie.
7.	Tu joues bien au tennis?	g.	Oui, j'aime Free Time.

4 | Answer the following questions based on the **Enquête culturelle** in **Leçon A**.

1. What are the names of two French fast-food restaurants?

   _____

   _____

2. What are some foods that most American and French teenagers like to eat?

   _____

   _____

3. What are the names of two American fast-food chains you can find in France?

   _____

   _____

4. When are the French more concerned about eating healthy foods?

   _____

   _____

5. What do the French often eat for dessert?

   _____

   _____

6. Do the French have any low-calorie foods in their supermarkets?

   _____

   _____

5 | Fill in each blank with the correct present tense form of the verb **aller**.

1. Comment _____-tu?

2. Nous _____ chez moi.

3. Ils _____ en boîte.

4. Vous _____ au cinéma?

5. On _____ au fast-food?

6. Je ne _____ pas au café.

6 | **A.** Draw the hands on each clock to match the time written below it.

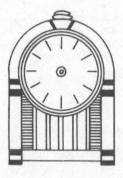

1. Il est dix heures.

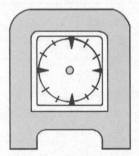

4. Il est midi.

3. Il est quatre heures.

2. Il est trois heures.

5. Il est neuf heures.

B. Write out the correct time in words for each clock or watch.

Modèle:

Il est neuf heures.

1. _____   5. _____

2. _____   6. _____

3. _____   7. _____

4. _____   8. _____

7 | The following is a portion of the train schedule from the Austerlitz train station in Paris to Tours, a city on the Loire River.

Numéro du train		50307	54029	4079	97023	4087	121	50162	4325	4325	185	50185	4031	54031	10123	4163	70123	4633	123	50123
Paris-Austerlitz	D		00.20			06.05	06.48		07.02	07.02	07.41		**07.51**		09.00			**09.03**	**09.30**	
Les Aubrais-Orléans	A		01.28			07.04			07.59	07.59			**08.48**					**10.00**		
Orléans	D			06.37	07.15											09.07				
Les Aubrais-Orléans	D		01.32						08.03	08.03			**08.50**					**10.25**		
Meung-sur-Loire	A			06.57					08.16	08.16						09.42		**10.37**		
Beaugency	A			07.05					08.22	08.22						09.54		**10.43**		
Mer (Loir-et-Cher)	A			07.14					08.31	08.31						10.07		**10.52**		
Blois	A		02.03	07.34	07.45				08.43	08.43						10.35		**11.03**		
Onzain	A			07.55						08.53								**11.20**		
Amboise	A			08.05						09.03								**11.31**		
St-Pierre-des-Corps	A	00.30	02.15	02.35		08.18	08.24	08.29	09.10	09.15	09.15	09.19	**09.43**	09.48	10.45	10.49		**11.44**	**11.08**	11.15
Tours	A	00.35	02.20	02.42		08.25		08.34	09.16	09.21	09.24		**09.53**			10.54		**11.50**		11.20

A – Arrivée   **D – Départ**

A. There are several express trains that leave from Paris-Austerlitz and don't stop again until St-Pierre-des-Corps. One express train that leaves Paris at 6:48 is referred to as number 121. Write down the numbers of the three other express trains and their departure times.

Train Number   **Departure Time**

1. _____   _____

2. _____   _____

3. _____   _____

B. Fill in the following chart according to the train schedule.

Departing From	Departure Time	Destination	Arrival Time
1. Paris	*6:05*	Orléans	7:15
2. Blois		Onzain	11:20
3. Les Aubrais-Orléans		Meung-sur-Loire	8:16
4. Orléans		Onzain	7:55
5. Blois		St-Pierre-des-Corps	2:35
6. Beaugency		Blois	7:34
7. Amboise		Tours	9:21
8. Mer (Loir-et-Cher)		Blois	10:35

8 Fill in the menu using food vocabulary from **Leçon B**.

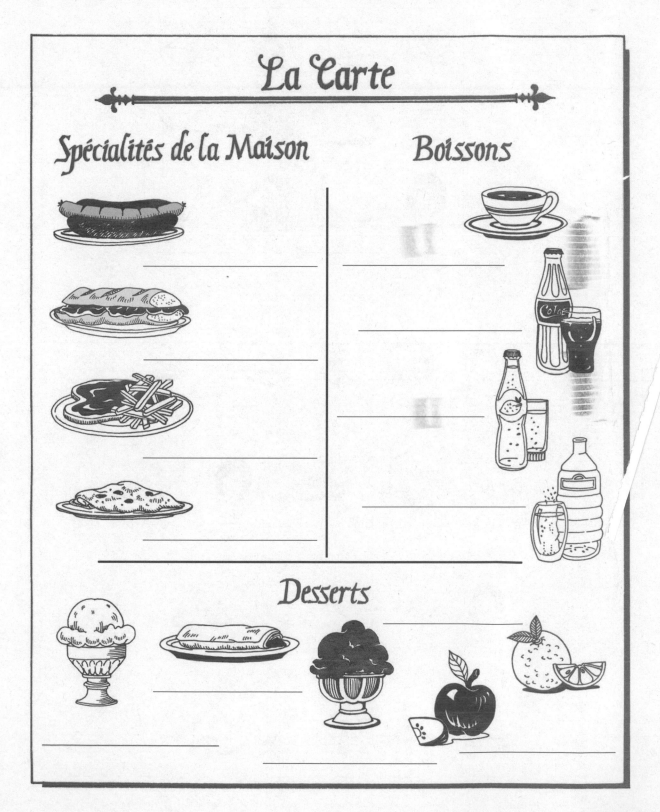

9 | **A.** Each of the following illustrations stands for a different letter. Use the letters represented by each illustration in the Key to help you figure out four words in the **Desserts** category.

Key:

1. ___ ___ ___ ___ ___

2. ___ ___ ___ ___ ___

3. ___ ___ ___ ___ ___

4. ___ ___ ___ ___ ___ ___ ___

B. Complete the crossword puzzle using the picture clues.

10 | The pictures below are out of order. Put them in sequence to make a meaningful conversation.

1.

3.

2.

4.

The sequence of scenes is: _____

11 Choose the best answer to each question from the following list and put its letter next to the question.

a. **le boulevard Saint-Michel**   e. **express**

b. Évian   f. crêpes

c. France   g. **la Sorbonne**

d. **diabolo menthe**   h. Belgium

_____ 1. What is France's most famous university called?

_____ 2. What is a dessert that comes from the province of Brittany?

_____ 3. What is one type of coffee that is made individually by the cup?

_____ 4. Where did French fries originate?

_____ 5. What street in Paris is the heart of the student quarter?

_____ 6. What beverage is made from lemon-lime soda and mint-flavored syrup?

_____ 7. What is a brand of mineral water?

12 According to the **Enquête culturelle** in **Leçon B**, the French drink certain beverages at specific times of the day. In English, compare the beverages your family drinks with what French people might drink in similar situations. Be sure to mention the differences that may exist between children, teens and adults.

_____

_____

_____

_____

_____

_____

_____

_____

_____

_____

13 | A. Circle the nouns and underline the verbs in the following list.

un café crème	une galette	nager
un jeu	dormir	une crêperie
téléphoner	un diabolo menthe	une friterie
une omelette	aller	une boisson
une eau minérale	regarder	une interro
sortir	un cinéma	
un vélo	préférer	

B. Label each of the pictures that follow. Remember to use **un** before a masculine noun and **une** before a feminine noun.

Modèle:

C'est un café.

4. _____

1. _____

5. _____

2. _____

6. _____

3. _____

7. _____

14 Look at the following ads for restaurants, then answer the questions.

LES ÉTOILES (crêperies), 20, rue du Débarcadère (17ᵉ). 01.45.72.59.39. Tlj. Sce jsq 1h du mat. Près du Palais des congrès, la gastronomie au service des crêpes et galettes, assiettes gourmandes, et salades copieuses. Carte env 12,20€ t.c.

RELAIS D'ÉGUISHEIM (Alsace), Place de la République (11ᵉ). 01.47.00.44.10. Tlj. Sce de 11h à 1h du matin. Belle brasserie, «crustacé de vermeil» avec fruits de mer, poissons du marché, choucroutes et autres spécialités alsaciennes. Terrasse fleurie. Carte env 27,44€. Menus 16,77 et 22,87€.
Spécialités des îles
Antilles - Île Maurice - Réunion

À TIPAZA (Nord Afrique), 155, rue St-Charles (15ᵉ). 01.45.54.01.17. Tlj. Sce jsq 23h. Une table orientale avec couscous, grillades au feu de bois, tagines et poissons. Carte env 19,82€ t.c. Formule à 11,89€.

ALSACE AUX HALLES
01.42.36.74.24. 16, rue Coquillière (1ᵉʳ) coquillages. Gde terrasse fleurie
OUVERT 24H SUR 24

LE PETIT GRUMEAU (crêperies), 54, Bd St Marcel (5ᵉ). 01.43.31.72.11. Tlj. Sce jsq 23h. Une crêperie pas comme les autres qui vous propose toutes sortes de galettes bretonnes, salades composées, glaces et cocktails. Menus 5,95 et 9,91€. Carte env 15,24€. Terrasse.

LA CRÊPERIE
(crêperies)
7, rue des Ciseaux (6ᵉ)
01.43.26.00.43. Tlj.
Une crêperie avec un grand choix de galettes blé noir et crêpes traditionnelles. Groupes sur réservation. Carte environ 13,72€ t.c. Formule plat du jour à 8,23€. Formule crêpes à 8,84 et 10,98€.

LE VENT DE SABLE (Nord Afrique), 31, rue Mademoiselle (15ᵉ). 01.48.28.03.49. Tlj. Sce jsq 23h. Joli restaurant au décor exotique, avec un large choix de couscous, des grillades au feu de bois et même des spécialités françaises. Carte env 18,29€ t.c.

LA CASE CRÉOLE
vous offre une cuisine authentique dans un joli décor
106, av. de Clichy (17ᵉ)
01.46.27.70.40
Ouv. tlj jsq 24h   M° Brochant

1. At which restaurant can you order **choucroute garni**?

   _____

2. At which three restaurants can you order specialties from Brittany?

   _____

   _____

3. Which two restaurants serve North African specialties?

   _____

4. At which restaurant can you order food from Martinique and Guadeloupe?

   _____

   _____

5. Which restaurants have an outside eating area?

   _____

   _____

6. Which two restaurants are open until 1:00 A.M.?

   _____

Leçon C

15 | Ça fait combien? Write out the price of each item.

Boissons

Café express	1,49€
Double express	2,58€
Café crème	3,05€
Cappuccino	3,96€
Coca	3,34€
Eau minérale	2,77€
Jus d'orange	3,20€
Jus de raisin	3,30€
Jus de pomme	3,23€
Milk-shake	4,62€
Citron pressé	3,81€

Modèle: Une eau minérale coûte *deux euros soixante-dix-sept.*

1. Un café express coûte _____

2. Un double express coûte _____

3. Un coca coûte _____

4. Un café crème coûte _____

5. Un jus de pomme coûte _____

6. Un cappuccino coûte _____

7. Un milk-shake coûte _____

8. Un citron pressé coûte _____

16 | Use the following pictures of French money to complete Activities 16A and 16B.

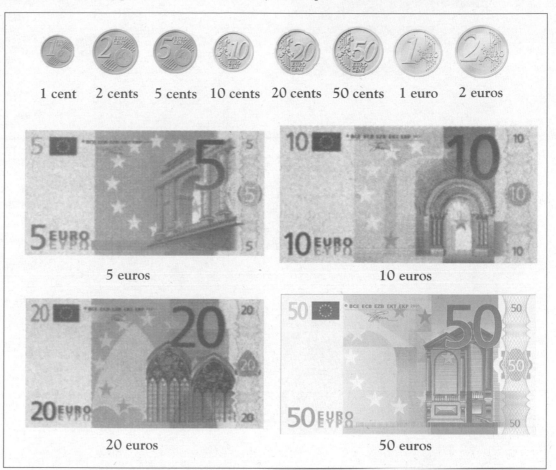

1 cent   2 cents   5 cents   10 cents   20 cents   50 cents   1 euro   2 euros

5 euros   10 euros

20 euros   50 euros

A. Fill in the price tag with the amount of money represented in each illustration.

1.

2.

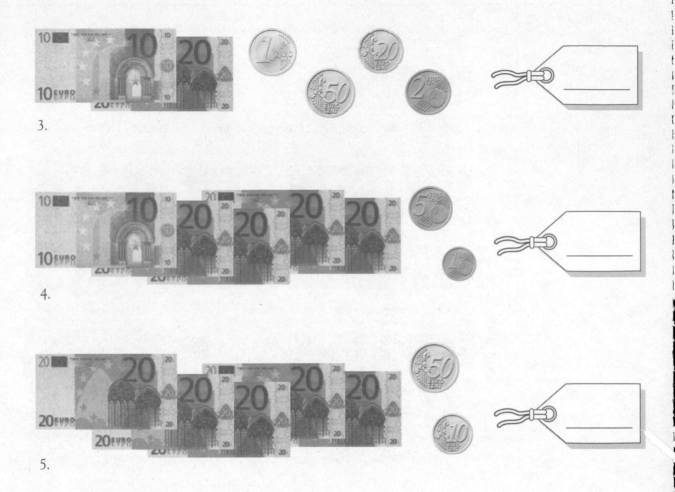

3. _____

4. _____

5. _____

B. Now imagine that you are writing a check. Write out in French words the total amount of money represented in each of the following illustrations.

1. _____

2. _____

3. _____

4. _____

5. _____

Now check your answers. The amount you have indicated in each price tag for Activity 16A should be the same as the amount you have written out in each answer for Activity 16B.

17 Imagine you want to eat lunch outside today. You could either buy something at **Le Goûter** and eat in the park, or you could sit outside and eat at **Le Café**. Look at the illustrations that follow and list the items sold only at **Le Goûter** in the circle on the left. Then list the items sold only at **Le Café** in the circle on the right. Finally, list the items sold at both **Le Goûter** and **Le Café** in the area where the two circles intersect. Be sure to write the appropriate definite article (**le, la** or **l'**) before the noun.

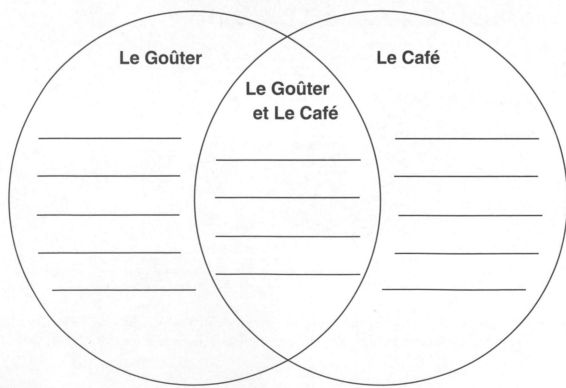

18 **A.** You are planning a picnic with some friends and need to gather together everything you want to take. In the space provided below each illustration, write what you already have.

Modèle:

Voilà les raisins.

4. _____

1. _____

5. _____

2. _____

6. _____

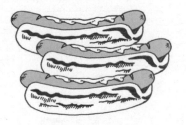

3. _____

7. _____

B. Using the menu on page 83 in your textbook, decide how much each of the following orders would cost. Use **Ils** or **Elles** and write out the numbers in words.

Modèle:

Ils coûtent six euros vingt-cinq.

3. _____

_____

1. _____

_____

4. _____

_____

2. _____

_____

5. _____

_____

19 **A.** Find at least 15 food cognates in this pizza menu and list them in French.

CHOISISSEZ VOTRE PIZZA OU COMPOSEZ-LA VOUS-MÊME.

Votre pizza est :

Préparée immédiatement après votre commande, à partir d'une pâte fraîche "slapée" à la main. Garnie avec des produits frais dont la qualité est un des tout premiers soucis.
Cuite dans un vrai four à pizza.
Emballée puis livrée chaude chez vous ou à votre bureau en moins de 30 minutes. Si jamais nous dépassions ce délai, nous vous rembourserions 1,52€

MENU		MOYENNE 1-2 PERS.	GRANDE 3-4 PERS.
		8,84€	12,50€
Provençale	Tomate, Fromage.	9,76€	13,72€
Américaine	Tomate, Fromage, Pepperoni.	9,76€	13,72€
Flambée	Crème fraîche, Oignons, Lardons.	10,67€	14,94€
Reine	Tomate, Fromage, Jambon, Champignons.	10,67€	14,94€
Soufflée	Tomate, Fromage, Lardons, Œufs.	11,59€	16,16€
Paysanne	Tomate, Fromage, Oignons, Saucisse, Lardons.	11,59€	16,16€
Végétarienne	(5 ingrédients au prix de 3). Tomate, Fromage, Oignons, Poivrons verts, Olives, Champignons, Double part de fromage.	12,50€	17,38€
Deluxe	(5 ingrédients au prix de 4). Tomate, Fromage, Oignons, Poivrons verts, Champignons, Pepperoni, Bœuf épicé.	13,42€	18,60€
Extravaganzza®	(9 ingrédients au prix de 5). Tomate, Fromage, Pepperoni, Oignons, Poivrons verts, Jambon, Champignons, Saucisse, Bœuf épicé, Double part de fromage, Olives.	0,91€	1,22€ Par garniture supplémentaire
En ajoutant à la Provençale votre choix de garnitures: Oignons, Poivrons verts, Champignons, Anchois, Double part de fromage, Jambon, Chorizo, Saucisse, Lardons, Thon, Ananas, Pepperoni, Bœuf épicé, Crème fraîche, Olives, Maïs, Œufs, Piments forts en rondelles.			0,91€

Coca-Cola ou Coca-Cola Light (33cl)

Piments gratuits sur demande

OFFRE SPÉCIALE*
1 Végétarienne moyenne
= 8,23€

OFFRE SPÉCIALE*
1 grande Végétarienne
=11,28€

01 44 09 09 99
12 rue du Général Lanrezac - Paris Étoile

EN 30 MIN. ELLE EST CHEZ VOUS.
LIVRAISON GRATUITE 7 JOURS SUR 7 DE 11H À 23H

B. Recognizing the cognates you have already found and using good detective skills, find three vegetables in the Deluxe pizza and list them in French.

_____

_____

_____

C. Imagine that you had the opportunity to invent your own pizza and add it to the menu. What ingredients would you include on your pizza? Follow the format from the preceding menu. Use your name as the name of the pizza and write your choice of ingredients in the space provided.

_____

_____

_____

_____

D. Using **J'aime beaucoup**, **J'aime bien**, **J'aime un peu** and **Je n'aime pas**, write eight sentences in French to explain the ingredients you chose to include (or not to include) in your pizza.

_____

_____

_____

_____

_____

_____

_____

_____

_____

_____

_____

_____

_____

_____

Unité 4   À l'école

Leçon A

1 | In the three parts of this activity, use the illustrations and the words **sur, derrière, devant, avec, dans** and **sous** to answer the questions.

A.

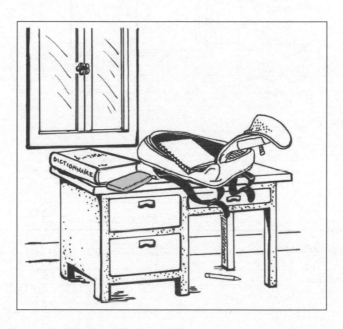

Modèle: Où est le sac à dos? *Le sac à dos est sur le bureau.*

1. Où est le crayon? _____

2. Où est la fenêtre? _____

3. Où est le cahier? _____

4. Où est le bureau? _____

5. Où est le dictionnaire? _____

6. Où est la trousse? _____

B.

1. Où est la télé? _____

2. Où est la stéréo? _____

3. Où est la vidéocassette? _____

4. Où est le CD? _____

5. Où est le magnétoscope? _____

6. Où est la cassette? _____

C.

C'EST À TOI!
Level One

1. Où est la corbeille? _____

2. Où est la carte? _____

3. Où est la feuille de papier? _____

4. Où est le bureau? _____

5. Où est l'ordinateur? _____

6. Où est le livre? _____

---

2 Answer the following questions according to the **Enquête culturelle** in **Leçon A**.

1. What do you carry in a **trousse**?

   _____

   _____

2. What do you carry in a **sac à dos**?

   _____

3. What might you say if you were disgusted with your grade on a test?

   _____

4. What might you say if you unexpectedly saw someone you knew in the hall at school?

   _____

5. How do many schools in France get their names?

   _____

   _____

6. Which word for "student" do high school students like to use to refer to themselves?

   _____

   _____

3 **A.** Tell what various people have by using the given subjects, the correct present tense form of the verb **avoir** and the name of the object from the corresponding number in the illustration. The first one has been done for you.

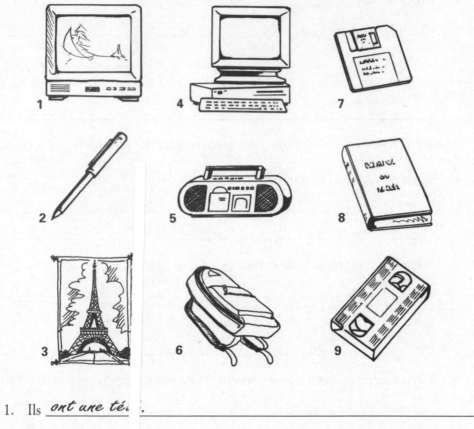

1. Ils _ont une té_____

2. Mme Garnier _____

3. Le prof _____

4. Marc et Cécile _____

5. Nous _____

6. On _____

7. Tu _____

8. Luc _____

9. Vous _____

B. Which of the items in Part A do you have? Write your answer in French.

_____

_____

4 | Complete each sentence with the correct form of **aller** or **avoir**.

Modèle: Christophe _____ *a* _____ un crayon.

1. Nous _____ un magnétoscope.
2. Je _____ au cinéma.
3. J' _____ trois stylos.
4. Les filles _____ un CD.
5. On y _____ ?
6. Nous _____ au café.
7. Pierre et Luc _____ chez moi.
8. Vous _____ une cassette de jazz.
9. Leïla _____ en boîte.
10. Tu _____ au fast-food?
11. Mlle Dherbey _____ un livre.
12. Tu _____ un ordinateur?

5 | Based on what you know about certain people, tell what they need. Use the expression **avoir besoin de (d')** and one of the illustrations to form each sentence.

Modèle: Nadia a une interro de maths demain.
Elle a besoin d'un livre de maths.

1. Marie a une feuille de papier.

_____

2. Georges et Alice ont une vidéocassette.

_____

3. M. et Mme Lescot vont en France.

_____

4. Pierre a soif.

_____

5. Céline a faim.

_____

6. Sandrine et Caroline désirent écouter de la musique.

_____

Leçon B

6 | Write out the following numbers in words.

Modèle: 999 *neuf cent quatre-vingt-dix-neuf*

1. 715 _____
2. 426 _____
3. 631 _____
4. 344 _____
5. 700 _____
6. 252 _____
7. 563 _____
8. 178 _____
9. 887 _____
10. 1000 _____

7 | In French, make a list of the classes you are taking now. Then tell how much you like each one, using **beaucoup, bien, un peu** and **ne (n')... pas.**

_____
_____
_____
_____
_____
_____
_____
_____
_____
_____
_____
_____

8 In the following classified ads people are offering their services as tutors in various subjects. Read the ads and then write down at least three telephone numbers you could call if you were interested in being tutored in each of the indicated courses.

COURS
- Étud. thèse de doctorat de maths donne cours tous niveaux pendant l'été. Tél. 01.48.13.67.26
- Français à dom. gramm., syntaxe, dictée, orth., rédact., rattrap. prononciat. Aussi débutants, tous âges. M. Diacond 01.48.05.21.58
- Professeur d'allemand longue expérience donne cours élèves et adultes. Tél. 01.45.75.67.64
- Prof. certifié exp. donne cours français, anglais, espagnol ts niveaux 9,15€ 1h30. Tél. 01.43.36.61.66
- Musique, cours de violon, guitare, piano, chant, basse élect., orgue, solfège, harmonic. Rapid, efficace. 01.42.03.62.50
- Français chez vous, orthographe, grammaire, prononciation, travail efficace. T. 01.47.97.74.43
- Élève classe préparatoire propose cours de maths de 6e à terminale. Tél. 01.43.76.77.69
- Toute traduction–espagnol, renseignements bienvenus au 01.47.60.30.27 ou ap. 20H 01.42.23.05.41
- Révisions intensives maths, physique, à Montparnasse par prof. expérimenté, exp. pédagogique 10 ans. Tél. 01.45.48.32.06
- Français, allemand: remise à niveau préparation examen par professeur. De bons résultats. 01.42.63.65.98

- Améliorez votre anglais avec un cours privé, tous niveaux. Tél. 01.45.20.25.88 (répondeur).
- Remise à niveau, (plus stages vacances juillet), maths, français, résumé. Enfant, adulte. Préparation examen. Efficacité assurée. 01.43.46.69.06
- Prof. d'espagnol (langue maternelle) donne cours rattrapage, intensif, examens. Tél. 01.45.02.99.54
- Prof. d'allemand (langue maternelle) donne cours rattrapage, intensif, examens. Tél. 01.45.20.99.45
- J. prof. de maths donne cours de maths, ts niv. prép. BAC concours, prox. Nation, juin, été. 01.43.79.15.68
- Rapid. American conversation. Ts nivx, cours d'anglais, ind. et pt. group. prof. USA dipl. 01.43.74.30.42
- Prof. britannique agrégé lycée et univ. donnerait cours d'anglais ts niveaux enf/adult. Jour, soir, Mo Denfert-Rochereau 15,24€/h. 01.46.33.79.43
- Ingénieur Centrale donne cours maths, physique, 30,49€/h. Messages au 01.46.34.26.69
- Étudiant diplômé de linguistique donne cours de français à étranger 12,20€/h. 01.43.02.58.79
- Prof. anglo. donne cours d'anglais à ts nivx et effectue ttes traductions. Tél. 24/24H 01.43.00.39.24

- Donne cours de rattrapage maths-phys. ts niv. Tél. 01.46.87.23.51. Laissez 1 mesg. si absent.
- Cours particuliers sur ordinateur, initiation, DOS, Word, dBASE, multi-plan. T. 01.48.62.62.01
- Guitare méthode simple et efficace accomp. blues, folk, picking. Pour renseignements. 01.43.44.63.14
- Professeur de maths donne cours 1ère S Term. C Deug IUT BTS Sup. Tél. 01.43.35.55.74 Montparnasse
- Cours individuel sur ordinateur, initiation, DOS, dBASE, traitements de texte. Tél. 01.43.46.17.79
- Guitare Folk Rock blues jazz rythme harmo impro, débutants bienvenus. Tél. 01.46.82.85.48
- Cours individuel sur ordinateur. Initiation à Lotus DOS Symphony Framework. 2 jours 228,67€. 01.47.53.70.27
- Professeur Maths sup. donne cours maths physique ts nvx à dom. 27,44€/h. Prépa exam. été. 01.42.55.87.03
- Espagnol trad. et cours tous niveaux (Bac. voyages trav. conv. univ.) Prof. hispanique. 01.47.73.63.47
- Prof. donne cours espagnol français, ts niveaux, suivi pédagogique. Tél. 01.45.33.99.78 ou 01.45.32.41.09

Les maths	La physique	L'informatique	La musique	Le français	L'allemand	L'anglais	L'espagnol

9 Without referring to your textbook, list in French as many items as you can that belong in the categories that follow. Then find a partner and compare your lists. Give yourself one point for each correctly spelled item on your list that is not on your partner's list. The partner with the most points wins!

Words on a Calendar	Languages	Electronic Equipment	Classroom Objects	School Subjects
_____	_____	_____	_____	_____
_____	_____	_____	_____	_____
_____	_____	_____	_____	_____
_____	_____	_____	_____	_____
_____	_____	_____	_____	_____

10 Select the best answer to each question according to the **Enquête culturelle** in **Leçon B**.

a. oui
b. mercredi
c. maths
d. non

e. lundi
f. si
g. philosophie
h. dimanche

i. samedi
j. jeudi

_____ 1. Do students in France have the same schedule every day of the week?

_____ 2. Unlike American students, on what day of the week do most French students have class?

_____ 3. Unlike American students, on what day of the week do most French students have very few classes or none at all?

_____ 4. Unlike American students, which subject do most French students take?

_____ 5. How do you answer "yes" to a negative question?

_____ 6. What is the first day of the week in France?

_____ 7. What is the first day of the week in Canada?

11 | **A.** Say what people are finishing by joining each subject in Column A with one of the nouns in Column B and using the correct form of the verb **finir**.

A		B
1. Valérie et Bruno		les devoirs
2. Émilie		le steak
3. Nous		la glace
4. Chantal et Yasmine	**finir**	les sandwichs
5. On		le livre
6. Vous		l'interro
7. Louis et Alexandre		le shopping

1. _____

2. _____

3. _____

4. _____

5. _____

6. _____

7. _____

B. Fill in the blank schedule with your own class schedule in French. Don't forget to include after-school activities.

EMPLOI DU TEMPS						
heures	**LUNDI**	**MARDI**	**MERCREDI**	**JEUDI**	**VENDREDI**	**SAMEDI**

12 | Write a sentence in English that defines or describes each of the following words or expressions.

1. Métro, boulot, dodo!

   _____

   _____

2. C.E.S.

   _____

   _____

3. le brevet des collèges

   _____

   _____

4. le baccalauréat

   _____

   la cantine

   _____

   _____

6. un goût

   _____

   _____

7. troisième

   _____

   _____

13 Answer the following questions according to the **Enquête culturelle** in **Leçon C**.

1. How is Patricia's Friday schedule different from yours?

   _____

2. How is Patricia's Monday schedule different from yours?

   _____

3. What are two occasions when the 24-hour clock might be used?

   _____

   _____

4. What is 9:00 P.M. in the 24-hour system?

   _____

5. What is **17h00** in the P.M. system?

   _____

6. How would a French speaker specify that it's 2:00 A.M.?

   _____

14 Using the 12-hour system, how would you ask a friend in French to go . . .

Modèle: to the school cafeteria at 12:45 P.M.?
   On va à la cantine à une heure moins le quart?

1. to school at 7:15 A.M.?

   _____

2. to the café at noon?

   _____

3. to the fast-food restaurant at 3:00 P.M.?

   _____

4. to your house at 4:30 P.M.?

   _____

5. to the movies at 7:45?

   _____

6. to the dance club at 10:00 P.M.?

   _____

15 Draw hands on each clock face to illustrate the time indicated. Then number the clocks in chronological order by writing the numbers "1" (for the earliest time) through "8" (for the latest time) on the lines provided.

_____ 1. Il est deux heures dix.

_____ 5. Il est deux heures et quart.

_____ 2. Il est deux heures moins dix.

_____ 6. Il est deux heures moins le quart.

_____ 3. Il est deux heures et demie.

_____ 7. Il est deux heures moins vingt.

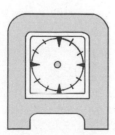

_____ 4. Il est deux heures vingt.

_____ 8. Il est deux heures.

16 | Write the correct time using the 24-hour system. A sun represents daytime and a moon represents nighttime.

 Modèle: 2:00   *Il est quatorze heures.* _____

 1. 3:00 _____

 2. 8:20 _____

 3. 10:35 _____

 4. 8:40 _____

 5. 9:55 _____

 6. 4:20 _____

 7. 11:15 _____

 8. 10:10 _____

 9. 9:30 _____

 10. 1:55 _____

 11. 9:45 _____

 12. 7:25 _____

13. 11:50 _____

17 **A.** **Le Printemps de Bourges** is an annual spring music festival that takes place in the city of Bourges in central France. Each year there are special **forfaits** (*ticket packages*) offered if you purchase three specific concert tickets. Use the concert schedule to fill in the chart for each of the **forfaits** offered on page 65. The first line of **Forfait A** has been done for you.

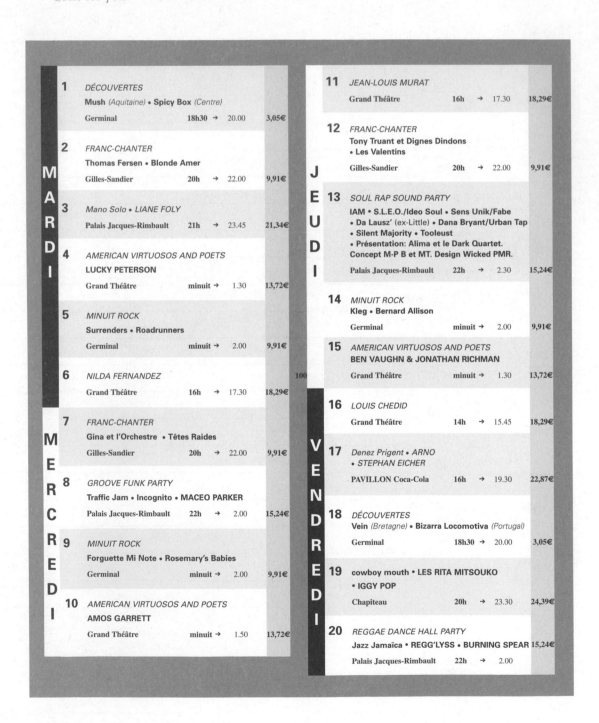

MARDI

1 *DÉCOUVERTES*
Mush *(Aquitaine)* • Spicy Box *(Centre)*
Germinal   18h30 → 20.00   3,05€

2 *FRANC-CHANTER*
Thomas Fersen • Blonde Amer
Gilles-Sandier   20h → 22.00   9,91€

3 *Mano Solo • LIANE FOLY*
Palais Jacques-Rimbault   21h → 23.45   21,34€

4 *AMERICAN VIRTUOSOS AND POETS*
LUCKY PETERSON
Grand Théâtre   minuit → 1.30   13,72€

5 *MINUIT ROCK*
Surrenders • Roadrunners
Germinal   minuit → 2.00   9,91€

6 *NILDA FERNANDEZ*
Grand Théâtre   16h → 17.30   18,29€

MERCREDI

7 *FRANC-CHANTER*
Gina et l'Orchestre • Têtes Raides
Gilles-Sandier   20h → 22.00   9,91€

8 *GROOVE FUNK PARTY*
Traffic Jam • Incognito • MACEO PARKER
Palais Jacques-Rimbault   22h → 2.00   15,24€

9 *MINUIT ROCK*
Forguette Mi Note • Rosemary's Babies
Germinal   minuit → 2.00   9,91€

10 *AMERICAN VIRTUOSOS AND POETS*
AMOS GARRETT
Grand Théâtre   minuit → 1.50   13,72€

JEUDI

11 *JEAN-LOUIS MURAT*
Grand Théâtre   16h → 17.30   18,29€

12 *FRANC-CHANTER*
Tony Truant et Dignes Dindons
• Les Valentins
Gilles-Sandier   20h → 22.00   9,91€

13 *SOUL RAP SOUND PARTY*
IAM • S.L.E.O./Ideo Soul • Sens Unik/Fabe
• Da Lausz' (ex-Little) • Dana Bryant/Urban Tap
• Silent Majority • Tooleust
• Présentation: Alima et le Dark Quartet.
Concept M-P B et MT. Design Wicked PMR.
Palais Jacques-Rimbault   22h → 2.30   15,24€

14 *MINUIT ROCK*
Kleg • Bernard Allison
Germinal   minuit → 2.00   9,91€

15 *AMERICAN VIRTUOSOS AND POETS*
BEN VAUGHN & JONATHAN RICHMAN
Grand Théâtre   minuit → 1.30   13,72€

VENDREDI

16 *LOUIS CHEDID*
Grand Théâtre   14h → 15.45   18,29€

17 *Denez Prigent • ARNO*
• STEPHAN EICHER
PAVILLON Coca-Cola   16h → 19.30   22,87€

18 *DÉCOUVERTES*
Vein *(Bretagne)* • Bizarra Locomotiva *(Portugal)*
Germinal   18h30 → 20.00   3,05€

19 *cowboy mouth • LES RITA MITSOUKO*
• IGGY POP
Chapiteau   20h → 23.30   24,39€

20 *REGGAE DANCE HALL PARTY*
Jazz Jamaïca • REGG'LYSS • BURNING SPEAR   15,24€
Palais Jacques-Rimbault   22h → 2.00

1. **Forfait A:** Concert #2 + #7 + #12=25€

Music Groups	Location	Day of the Week	Time	Price
Thomas Ferson, Blonde Amer	*Gilles-Sandier*	*mardi*	*vingt heures à vingt-deux heures*	*9,91€*

2. **Forfait B:** Concert #5 + #9 + #14=25€

Music Groups	Location	Day of the Week	Time	Price

3. **Forfait C:** Concert #6 + #11 + #16=48€

Music Groups	Location	Day of the Week	Time	Price

B. How much money would you save by buying each **forfait** package, instead of purchasing the tickets separately? Refer to the information on pages 64 and 65 to calculate the savings.

	Forfait A	Forfait B	Forfait C
Savings:			

---

18 Use the illustrations, titles, context and cognates in the following back-to-school ads to write the French equivalents of the words or expressions.

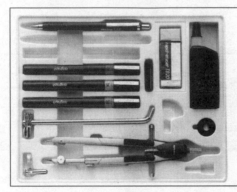

College Set 530 326 avec
3 stylos à encre de Chine isograph,
largeurs de trait 0,2–0,35–0,7 mm
1 flacon d'encre de Chine 23 ml
1 gomme crayon/encre de Chine TB 20
1 porte-mine calibré Tikky T 0,5
1 grand compas à vis centrale, réglage
rapide et verge de rallonge
1 attache-compas ø 3,5/4 mm
1 tube de mines

Gabarit de cercles
Cercles de ø 1,0 – 30 mm avec pro-
gression de 1 mm en 1 mm.
Rayons 4, 6, 10, 16 mm. Graduation
en mm. Avec
alvéole de levage.
840 631 ☛
255 x 92 x 1,6 mm
Instruments de
dessin: ∪ 0,5 m V

Règles triangulaires de réduction
avec graduations de réduction adaptées
à la pratique. En plastique blanc de
qualité supérieure,
2 gorges en couleur.
802 019–802 024

1. compass _____

2. circles _____

3. plastic _____

4. quality _____

5. rulers _____

6. small bottle _____

7. ink _____

8. eraser (for pencil and ink) _____

Unité 5 *En famille*

1 **A.** According to the family tree, answer each of the following questions in a complete sentence.

Modèle: Qui est l'enfant de Stéphanie?
Marie est l'enfant de Stéphanie.

1. Qui est la mère de Marie?

   _____

2. Qui est le père de Marie?

   _____

3. Qui est la mère de Robert?

_____

4. Qui est le père de Stéphanie?

_____

5. Qui est la mère de Guy?

_____

6. Qui est le beau-père de Robert?

_____

7. Qui est la fille de Stéphanie et Guy?

_____

Qui est la fille de Béatrice et André?

_____

9. Qui est le beau-frère de Marie?

_____

10. Qui est la femme de Théo?

_____

11. Qui est le mari de Céline?

_____

12. Qui est la belle-mère de Céline?

_____

B. Fill in the blanks with the appropriate relationships according to the family tree in Part A.

Modèle: André est _____ *le grand-père* _____ de Marie.

1. Béatrice est _____ de Stéphanie.

2. Nadine est _____ de Marie.

3. Théo est _____ de Marie.

4. André est _____ de Béatrice.

5. Guy est _____ de Théo.

6. Marie est _____ de Robert.

7. Céline est _____ de Guy.

8. Céline est _____ de Marie.

2 Answer the following questions according to the **Enquête culturelle** in **Leçon A**.

1. What is the purpose of proverbs?

   _____

2. What is the French equivalent of the proverb "Like father, like son"?

   _____

3. In general, what does this proverb imply?

   _____

4. How would you say "stepson" and "stepdaughter" in French?

   _____

5. How would you say "father-in-law" and "mother-in-law" in French?

   _____

6. If the French term for "daughter-in-law" is **belle-fille**, what is the French term for "son-in-law"?

   _____

   _____

3 **A.** Fill in each blank using the possessive adjective **son**, **sa** or **ses**.

Voilà le bureau de Barbara. Sur _____ bureau elle a _____ dictionnaire, _____ ordinateur et une photo de _____ grand-mère. Barbara aime écouter de la musique. Alors, derrière _____ bureau elle a _____ stéréo et _____ cassettes. _____ sac à dos est sur _____ chaise. Dans _____ sac à dos elle a _____ livres, _____ trousse et _____ cahier.

B. Mathieu is at the library with his two little brothers and Alice is there with her little sister. They are getting ready to leave and are making sure everyone has their belongings. Fill in the blanks in the conversation with the appropriate possessive adjectives.

Mathieu: _____ sœur a _____ crayons et _____ cahier?

Alice: Oui. Et _____ frères ont _____ dictionnaire et _____ sacs à dos?

Mathieu: Oui. Tu as _____ cahier et _____ livres?

Alice: J'ai _____ livres, mais je n'ai pas _____ cahier.

Mathieu: Voilà _____ cahier.

Alice: Merci. Et _____ frères et toi, vous avez _____ trousses?

Mathieu: Oui, voilà _____ trousses. Tu as _____ trousse?

Alice: Oui, dans _____ sac à dos.

4 | Describe the appearance of two of your classmates in French, in as much detail as possible. Include their ages, the color of their hair and the color of their eyes. Read your descriptions out loud to another classmate. Ask him or her to guess whom you described.

Classmate 1:

_____

_____

_____

_____

_____

_____

_____

Classmate 2:

_____

_____

_____

_____

_____

_____

_____

5 Fill in the blank with the name of the appropriate month for each calendar page.

			1	2	3
4	5	6	7	8	9	10
11	12	13	♥	15	16	17
18	19	20	21	22	23	24
25	26	27	28

1. _____

1	2	3		5	6
7	8	9	10	11	12	13
14	15	16	17	18	19	20
21	22	23	24	25	26	27
28	29	30	31

4. _____

	2	3	4	5	6
7	8	9	10	11	12	13
14	15	16	17	18	19	20
21	22	23	24	25	26	27
28	29	30	31

2. _____

					1	2
3	4	5	6	7	8	9
10	11	12	13	14	15	16
17	18	19	20	21	22	23
24	25	26	27		29	30

5. _____

			1	2	3
4	5	6	7	8	9	10
11	12	13	14	15	16	
18	19	20	21	22	23	24
25	26	27	28	29	30	31

3. _____

	1	2	3	4	5
6	7	8	9	10	11	12
13	14	15	16	17	18	19
20	21	22	23	24	25	26
27	28	29	30	

6. _____

6 | **A.** Use the illustrations to help you fill in the crossword puzzle.

B. Write a few sentences in French about your pet or a friend's or relative's pet. Think about the following questions as you write: What kind of pet is it? What is the pet's name? How old is the pet? What color are the pet's eyes?

_____

_____

_____

_____

_____

7 **A.** Look through the following ads for pets to be adopted. Then answer the questions.

◆ **Vds BB caniche nain ou Toy et BB Cocker tat vacc, gar véto, liv poss fac de paiem. Tél. 01 45.09.67.20**

◆ À vendre poissons africains Haplocromis crisonotus 4 cm, parent visible, bleu électrique. Tél. 01.48.54.01.82 ap 18H

◆ Chiots caniche, yorkshire, bichon, shih tzu, pékinois, teckel, pincher, spitz, labrador, basset hound, boxer, beauceron, husky, doberman, berger allem.-montagne Pyrén. + croisés. 01.48.83.27.52

◆ Jeune chat cherche foyer, vacc, tatoué Tél. 01.47.22.43.30

◆ Donne chat gris 1 an, et chatte noire 8 mois, très câline, opérés et tatoués avec suivi. 01.42.32.02.25

◆ Donne ctre bons soins chatte noire 5 mois, chaton noir 1 mois Tél. 01.46.72.66.03

1. What phone number might you call if you had an aquarium?

   _____

2. What phone number might you call if you wanted to adopt a Labrador retriever?

   _____

3. What two phone numbers might you call if you wanted to adopt a black cat?

   _____

4. What phone number might you call if you were interested in a Shih Tzu?

   _____

5. What phone number might you call if you were interested in a cocker spaniel?

   _____

B. Write out in words the approximate population of each of the following French-speaking countries, regions or cities.

1. France (57.800.000) _____

2. Martinique (360.000) _____

3. Quebec (6.896.000) _____

4. Senegal (6.982.000) _____

5. Vietnam (64.412.000) _____

6. Marseille (1.231.000) _____

7. Lille (959.000) _____

8. Limoges (170.000) _____

8 Read the answer in each of the following categories and then write the question.

History and Geography	Overseas Departments	Metric System	Animals
1. It is located near the mouth of the Loire.	4. They are two French overseas departments.	7. It was developed by a commission of French scientists.	10. They are all services that target pets.
2. It gave some religious freedoms to the Huguenots.	5. The capital is Fort-de-France.	8. It was first used in the 1790s.	11. They are welcome in hotels, stores and restaurants.
3. It is the name of the religion practiced by the Huguenots.	6. She was born in Martinique.	9. It is shorter than a mile.	12. They keep the city's sidewalks clean.

1. _____

2. _____

3. _____

4. _____

5. _____

6. _____

7. _____

8. _____

9. _____

10. _____

_____

11. _____

12. _____

9 | Write complete sentences using a subject from Column A, a form of **être** and an expression from Column B.

	A		**B**
1.	Tu		dans la cantine
2.	Monique		à l'école
3.	Nous		avec Thierry
4.	Alain et Gilles	**être**	ensemble
5.	Je		au café
6.	Anne-Marie		professeur
7.	Vous		au cinéma
8.	Marcel		en vacances

1. _____

2. _____

3. _____

4. _____

5. _____

6. _____

7. _____

8. _____

10 | Complete each sentence with the correct form of **avoir**, **être** or **aller**.

1. Sa sœur _____ treize ans.

2. Vous _____ sympa.

3. J' _____ un chien.

4. Tu _____ beau.

5. David _____ à la Martinique dimanche.

6. Jeanne _____ deux sœurs.

7. On y _____ ?

8. Marie et Anne _____ les cousines de Véronique.

9. C' _____ quelle date?

10. M. et Mme Dupont _____ en vacances demain.

12 | **A.** Use the diagram that follows to show similarities and differences between families in the United States and France. In the circle labeled "France," write some characteristics of families in France. In the circle labeled "U.S.," do the same for families in the United States. Then write similarities in the area where the two circles intersect. Compare your answers with a classmate's.

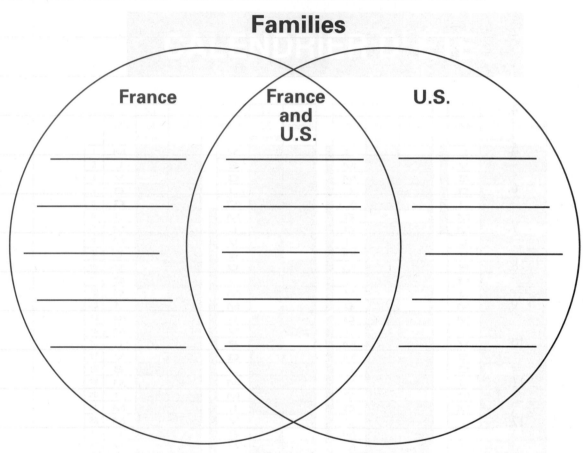

Families

France

France and U.S.

U.S.

B. Use the information in your diagram to write at least three sentences in English comparing and contrasting French and American family life.

_____

_____

_____

_____

_____

_____

_____

_____

13 | Draw pictures or place photographs of your family members in each box. Then tell how each person is related to you and use two adjectives to describe his or her personality.

Modèle:

C'est mon père.

Il est diligent et intelligent.

1. _____

_____

_____

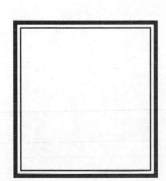

3. _____

_____

_____

2. _____

_____

_____

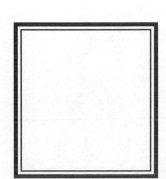

4. _____

_____

_____

14 | Fill in the blank with the opposite of each word or expression.

1. diligent   _____
2. méchant   _____
3. généreux   _____
4. bête   _____
5. timide   _____

6. bavarde   _____
7. égoïste   _____
8. sympa   _____
9. paresseuse   _____
10. intelligente   _____

15 | Use a subject, a form of **être** and an appropriate adjective to describe the person or people in each picture. Be sure that each adjective agrees with the subject it is describing!

Modèle:

La fille est généreuse.

1. _____

2. _____

3. _____

4. _____

5. _____

16 | Use the correct form of **beau** to describe each of the following illustrations.

Modèle:

Voilà une belle prof.

3. _____

1. _____

4. _____

2. _____

5. _____

17 Using any words you already know in French, plus cognates, contextual clues and your own cultural experience, answer the questions about the following French wedding invitations.

La Baronne Lelarge d'Ervau,
La Comtesse Hersart de la Villemarqué
de Cornouaille,
Le Baron et la Baronne Guy Lelarge d'Ervau
sont heureux de vous faire part du mariage de
Mademoiselle Sophie Lelarge d'Ervau, leur petite-
fille et fille, avec Monsieur Olivier de Guibert.

Et vous invitent à participer ou à vous unir par la
prière à la messe de mariage qui sera célébrée le samedi 11 mai
2002, à 15 heures, en l'église de Nizon (Pont-Aven), par
l'Abbé Roland Hersart de la Villemarqué de Cornouaille, oncle
de la mariée.

Le consentement des époux sera reçu par l'Abbé
Max de Guibert, cousin du marié.

2, rue Chauvin 44000 Nantes
Brassioux, Monthoiron 86210 Bonneuil Matours
49, boulevard de Glatigny 78000 Versailles

Madame Max de Guibert,
Le Docteur et Madame Luc Bianchi,
Monsieur et Madame Patrice de Guibert
sont heureux de vous faire part du mariage de
Monsieur Olivier de Guibert, leur petit-fils et fils, avec
Mademoiselle Sophie Lelarge d'Ervau.

Et vous invitent à participer ou à vous unir par la
prière à la messe de mariage qui sera célébrée le samedi 11 mai
2002, à 15 heures, en l'église de Nizon (Pont-Aven), par
l'Abbé Roland Hersart de la Villemarqué de Cornouaille, oncle
de la mariée.

Le consentement des époux sera reçu par l'Abbé
Max de Guibert, cousin du marié.

Le Fort 44150 Saint-Herblon
4, rue des Capucins 29800 Landerneau

---

1. What is the difference between these two invitations?

   _____

   _____

2. What is the bride's name?

   _____

3. What is the groom's name?

   _____

4. What is the date of the wedding?

   _____

5. What time will the wedding take place?

   _____

6. Is this an invitation to a wedding at **la mairie** or at a church?

   _____

7. What word or words give you the answer to Question 6?

   _____

   _____

8. What are the names of the parents and the grandparents of the bride?

   _____

   _____

   _____

9. What are the names of the parents and the grandparents of the groom?

   _____

   _____

   _____

10. Who is the uncle of the bride?

    _____

    _____

11. Who is the cousin of the groom?

    _____

12. What is the French word for "bride"?

    _____

13. What is the French word for "groom"?

    _____

Unité 6   *Tu viens d'où?*

1   In French, list the names of the countries you know that are located in each continent shown on the maps below: **l'Asie**, **l'Europe** and **l'Amérique du Nord**. Be sure to include the definite article **le**, **la**, **l'** or **les** with the name of each country.

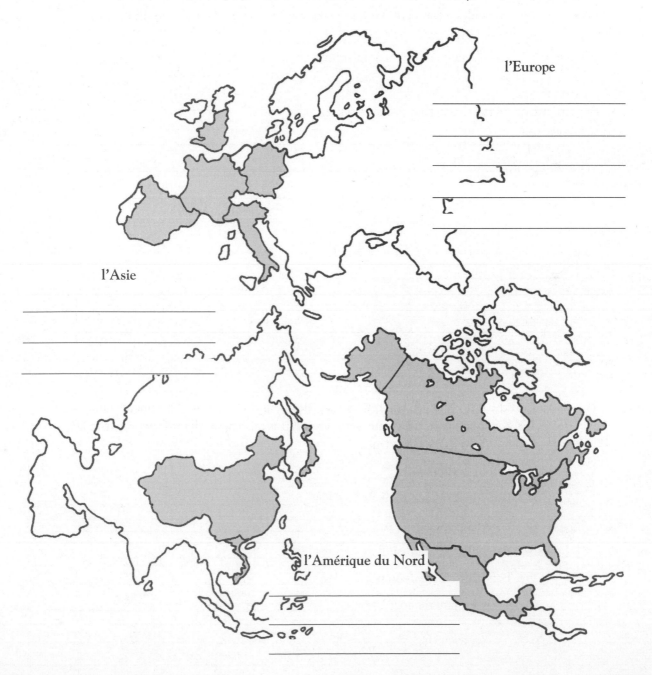

l'Europe

_____

_____

_____

_____

l'Asie

_____

_____

_____

l'Amérique du Nord

_____

_____

_____

2 | **A.** As Betsy, Peter and Angelika looked at pictures and talked, a friend transcribed their conversation. Somehow the transcript got all mixed up!

Peter: Nous venons d'Angleterre. Mes frères, mon père et moi, nous sommes anglais. Ma mère est canadienne. Et toi, Angelika, tu viens d'où?

Betsy: Qui est sur la photo?

Angelika: Et ta famille et toi, Peter, vous venez d'où?

Peter: Ce sont mes parents et mes frères.

Betsy: Tu ressembles à ton père. Moi, je ressemble à ma mère. Je viens des États-Unis. Je suis de Chicago.

Angelika: Je viens d'Allemagne. Voilà une photo de ma famille.

Rewrite the conversation so that it makes sense.

1. _____

2. _____

3. _____

_____

4. _____

5. _____

_____

_____

6. _____

B. Now read the conversation you rewrote and decide if the following statements are true or false. If the statement is true, write **V** for **vrai**. If it is false, write **F** for **faux**. Rewrite any false statements to make them true.

_____ 1. Peter est allemand. _____

_____ 2. La mère de Peter vient du Canada. _____

_____ 3. Son père est canadien. _____

_____ 4. Angelika est allemande. _____

_____ 5. Betsy ressemble à son père. _____

_____ 6. Betsy est américaine. _____

3 | Answer the following questions according to the **Enquête culturelle** in **Leçon A**.

1. On what river is Tours located?

   _____

2. Why might tourists visit Tours?

   _____

3. Why are there many students in Tours?

   _____

   _____

4. Why do Europeans often travel to neighboring countries?

   _____

   _____

5. What do European tourists like to do when they visit neighboring countries?

   _____

   _____

6. Why do Europeans find it crucial to learn a second language?

   _____

   _____

4 | Claude is organizing a get-together with some friends at a local café to begin at 6:30. Some will be late and others (indicated by "—") can't come at all. Write a sentence saying when the following people are coming.

Modèle: Marc / 6h30   *Marc vient à 6h30.*

1. Robert et Charles / 7h15 _____
2. Karine et toi / 6h30 _____
3. Khalid / 6h45 _____
4. Sandra et Delphine / 7h00 _____
5. Anne-Laure / — _____
6. Didier et moi / 6h30 _____
7. Céline et Patrick / — _____
8. Je / 6h30 _____

5 Write complete sentences using a subject from Column A, a present tense form of the verb **venir** and a word or phrase from Column B. The first one is done for you.

	A		B
1.	Nous		ensemble
2.	Vous		d'Allemagne
3.	Pablo		des États-Unis
4.	Je		chez moi
5.	Rubén et María	**venir**	avec nos parents
6.	Sandrine		à six heures
7.	Tu		d'Espagne
8.	On		du Mexique
9.	Elles		de l'école
10.	Lisa et Cathy		demain

1. *Nous venons avec nos parents.*
2. _____
3. _____
4. _____
5. _____
6. _____
7. _____
8. _____
9. _____
10. _____

6 Use the name of the country pictured and a form of the verb **venir** to write a sentence telling where each of the following people comes from.

Modèle:

Je *viens de France.* _____

1. Ana et moi, nous _____

5. Tu _____

2. Keiko _____

6. Maria et Sofia _____

3. Vous _____

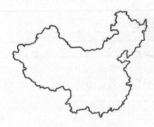

7. Li _____

4. Derek _____

8. Diem et Nyen _____

7 | **A.** Write to your French pen pal, Jean-Michel, and ask him the following questions.

1. Do you eat at school?

_____

2. Do you study Spanish?

_____

3. Do you like to watch movies?

_____

4. Do you look like your mother or your father?

_____

5. Do you play basketball?

_____

B. Now try to learn more about Jean-Michel by asking . . .

1. what he likes to do.

_____

2. how he goes to school.

_____

3. at what time he goes to school.

_____

4. what he likes to study.

_____

5. why he is studying English.

_____

Leçon B

8 │ In French, list the professions of some of the people who are likely to work at each of the
following places. Try to think of two different occupations in each case.

De la 4ème aux Classes Terminales

Cours et Institut Charlemagne

→ consultez l'Annuaire Électronique
Nom COURS CHARLEMAGNE
Loc PARIS
Dept 75

Externat Demi pension, Mixte
Horaires renforcés, Encadrement strict.
Contrôle hebdomadaire des connaissances.
Initiation à l'Informatique.

Cours de vacances et de soutien accessibles à
des élèves EXTÉRIEURS

COURS CHARLEMAGNE   INSTITUT CHARLEMAGNE
ENSEIGNEMENT SECONDAIRE PRIVÉ

1. _____
_____

Scoot Informatique
4, rue Jean Rostand
ZAC des Vignes - Parc club ORSAY UNIVERSITÉ
91893 ORSAY CEDEX

Système de gestion, de facturation, de
comptabilité de stocks et de paie
pour PME, PMI

Fonctionnant sous UNIX et réseau
spécifique à la demande, pour adapter
Scoot à votre entreprise
Prix compétitif

2. _____
_____

CENTRE HÔPITALIER STE-ANNE

→ consultez l'Annuaire Électronique
Nom CENTRE HÔPITALIER STE-ANNE   *ou 3614 code Hôpital Ste-Anne*
Loc PARIS
Dept 75

STANDARD - 1, rue Cabanis - 75674 PARIS
CPOA - même adresse
Centre Virginie Olivier - Centre de formation
Crèche : 5ter, rue d'Alésia

3. _____
_____

CÔTE D' AZUR DENTAIRE

CÔTE D´AZUR DENTAIRE

Équipement Dentaire Fourniture

4. _____

_____

L'Albergo

HÔTEL - RESTAURANT * NN

Chambres tout confort - Cadre agréable - calme
Téléphone direct - Parking privé

5. _____

_____

Anny
HAUTE COIFFURE

Coiffure mixte
Manucure

Demandez Nicole

Journée continue
vendredi et samedi

6. _____

_____

**Union
de Banques
Régionales
U.B.R.**
pour le crédit
industriel

7. _____

_____

9 Answer the following questions according to the **Enquête culturelle** in **Leçon B**.

1. How old must a person be to work full-time in France?

   _____

   _____

2. How long is the official work week in France?

   _____

   _____

3. How many weeks of vacation a year do salaried employees receive?

   _____

   _____

4. May salaried workers take all their vacation time at once?

   _____

   _____

5. How many paid holidays do salaried workers get per year?

   _____

6. What continuing education courses do many French workers take?

   _____

   _____

10 Write five complete sentences on page 95 to tell what Djamel has and Marc does not have. Then write six sentences to tell what Marc has and Djamel does not have.

Modèle: *Djamel a des chiens.*
               Marc n'a pas de chiens.

1. _____
_____

2. _____
_____

3. _____
_____

4. _____
_____

5. _____
_____

6. _____
_____

7. _____
_____

8. _____
_____

9. _____
_____

10. _____
_____

11. _____
_____

11 For each of the following statements, ask two questions to obtain more specific information using a form of **quel**.

Modèle: Le prof parle à ses élèves.

Quel prof parle à ses élèves?

Le prof parle à quels / quelles élèves?

1. La fille va en boîte avec ses cousines.

_____

_____

2. L'enfant regarde le cheval.

_____

_____

3. L'élève fait ses devoirs.

_____

_____

4. La coiffeuse mange au café.

_____

_____

5. La comptable travaille avec les informaticiennes.

_____

_____

12 | Claire and her friend Annick are describing photos of their families to one another. Complete their conversations with **c'est, ce sont, il est, elle est, ils sont** or **elles sont**.

1.

Claire: Voilà mon père. _____ prof dans une école à Tokyo.

Annick: Ah, _____ japonais, ton père?

Claire: Mais non! _____ français. Et voilà ma mère. _____ japonaise. _____ de Tokyo.

Annick: Et les trois filles?

Claire: _____ mes sœurs.

2.

Annick: Voilà mes cousins, Peter et Tony. _____ de Londres. _____ anglais. Et voilà leur père. _____ de Munich.

Claire: _____ ton oncle Kurt? _____ allemand? Et qui est la femme?

Annick: _____ la mère de mes cousins, ma tante Jane.

Claire: _____ la sœur de ta mère?

Annick: Oui. _____ anglaise.

13 Write each of the names that follow in the appropriate column. Be careful—there may be more lines than you need!

le Jura / Bordeaux / la Seine / les Alpes / le Rhône / les Vosges / Calais / la Garonne /

le Massif Central / Biarritz / Deauville / la Loire / Étretat / Saint-Malo / les Pyrénées /

Le Havre / Marseille / Toulon / le Rhin / Paris

Mountains	Cities	Rivers
_____	_____	_____
_____	_____	_____
_____	_____	_____
_____	_____	_____
_____	_____	_____
_____	_____	_____
_____	_____	_____
_____	_____	_____
_____	_____	_____

14   In French, describe what the weather might be like in each place during the specified season. Use each weather expression only once.

    Modèle: à Chicago, Illinois, au printemps   *Il fait du vent.* _____

    1.   à Vail, Colorado, en hiver _____

    2.   à Dallas, Texas, en été _____

    3.   à Washington, D.C., au printemps _____

    4.   à Portland, Oregon, au printemps _____

    5.   à Minneapolis, Minnesota, en hiver _____

    6.   à Cleveland, Ohio, en automne _____

    7.   à Rochester, New York, en hiver _____

    8.   à Mobile, Alabama, en été _____

15   Using the illustrations as a clue, complete each sentence to explain what the following people are doing.

    Modèle:

Je *fais du footing.* _____

1. Vous _____

2. Les garçons _____

3. Nous _____

4. Je _____

5. Sophie _____

6. Marc _____

7. Tu _____

16 | Rewrite the following questions using inversion.

Modèle: Vous aimez les frites, n'est-ce pas?

Aimez-vous les frites?

1. Est-ce que vous voyagez beaucoup?

   _____

2. Vous nagez en hiver?

   _____

3. Ils ont une stéréo, n'est-ce pas?

   _____

4. Est-ce qu'ils ont un chien?

   _____

5. Il est intelligent, n'est-ce pas?

   _____

6. Est-ce que vous avez des frères?

   _____

7. Pourquoi est-ce qu'elle joue au tennis?

   _____

8. À quelle heure est-ce qu'elles viennent?

   _____

9. Avec qui est-ce qu'il danse?

   _____

10. Quand est-ce que tu manges au fast-food?

   _____

11. Quel livre est-ce qu'il a?

   _____

12. Où est-ce que tu vas?

   _____

17 | **A.** Skim the listings that follow to learn what kinds of things are being advertised. Write an appropriate heading in English for each column.

1. _____

la vraie raclette montagnarde
LE BOUCHON DU MARAIS
raclette à volonté :12,20€
Fondue Bourg. garnie : 12,50€ · Savoy. : 10,52€

LE DAUPHIN
Bouillabaisse, Ris de veau, Confits
Menus 18,29€ et 25,25€ s.c. et carte. Fermé dimanche
Toutes cartes de crédit acceptées

EL BURRIQUITO
Restaurant Espagnol
DÎNER SPECTACLE
Ambiance typique avec musiciens
Service jusqu'à 4 h du matin. Salle cli. - Groupes acceptés

BISTROT
SAVOYARD
FONDUES ● RACLETTE
MAGRET de Canard ● POTÉE savoyarde
Toutes les pièces de bœuf

2. _____

ÉGLISE DE LA MADELEINE
Mardi 30 juin à 20h30
IXᵉ SYMPHONIE de BEETHOVEN

27 juin à 21h
GYMNASE de L'ALMONT à MELUN
9ᵉ de Beethoven
ORCHESTRE SYMPHONIQUE **AMA-DEUS**

TORONTO CHILDREN'S CHORUS
Le célèbre chœur d'enfants canadien
dirigé par Jean Ashworth Bartle
Cathédrale AMÉRICAINE : 26 juin, 20h30
Cathédrale de CHARTRES : 27 juin, 20h30
FESTIVAL D'AUVERS : 28 juin, 17h30

CHAQUE JOUR EN SORBONNE
DU 22 JUIN AU 5 JUILLET
CONCERTS
MUSIQUES SLAVES
Réservations : 01.42.62.71.71
FNAC - VIRGIN - 17 rue de la Sorbonne

3. _____

C BEETHOVEN – Amér., coul. (92). Comédie, de Brian Levant : Un Saint-Bernard, échappé du chenil, fait la loi dans la famille qu'il s'est choisi, en imposant même à son maître, un PDG stressé qui ne l'accueillait qu'avec réticence. Avec Charles Grodin, Bonnie Hunt, Dean Jones, Nicholle Tom, Christopher Castile, Sarah Rose Carr, Oliver Platt, Stanley Tucci.

O BELLE HISTOIRE (LA) (2000 ans de galère pour une seconde d'éternité) – Franç., coul. (91). Aventure intemporelle, de Claude Lelouch : La plus belle des histoires ? Une histoire d'amour - le coup de foudre qui, de façon inexplicable et de tous temps, a frappé des êtres qui, l'espace de quelques instants, se prennent presque pour des dieux. Avec Gérard Lanvin, Béatrice Dalle, Vincent Lindon, Marie-Sophie L, Patrick Chesnais, Gérard Darmon. **Parnassiens 14e.**

J ◆ BLANCHE NEIGE ET LES 7 NAINS (Snow White and the seven dwarfs) – Amér., coul. (37). Dessin animé, de Walt Disney : Seul le Prince Charmant peut sortir Blanche Neige du profond sommeil dans lequel l'a plongée sa belle-mère, une méchante sorcière. D'après le conte des frères Grimm. **Club Gaumont - Publicis Matignon 8e, Denfert 14e, Saint-Lambert 15e.**

4. _____

BOWLINGS :
Bowling de Paris, Jardin d'Acclimatation, Bois de Boulogne.
Bowling de Montparnasse, 27, rue du Cdt-Mouchotte.   M° Montparnasse.
4 Bowlings Sympa, Bowling de la Chapelle, La Défense, 1 de la Chapelle, La Défense, Champerret, Front de Seine. 72 pistes avec autoscores ou téléscores.

CANOË-KAYAK :
Point Rivière, location canoës et kayaks, cours, stages, W.E. randonnées en Île de France et autres régions. Rens.

CYCLISME :
Bicyclub, 7 centres de location de bicyclettes en Île-de-France : Bois de Boulogne, Bois de Vincennes, Canal de l'Ourcq, Vallée de Chevreuse, St-Germain-en-Laye, Fontainebleau et Rambouillet. Ouvert sam., dim. et jours fériés de 9h à 19h, jusqu'au 24 novembre (Bois de Boulogne et Fontainebleau ouvert aussi tlj en juillet-août). Tarifs à l'heure, à la journée ou à la semaine. Rens.

GOLF MINIATURE :
Châlet du Lac, Orée du bois de Vincennes, M° Saint-Mandé-Tourelles, 01 43 28 09 89. Ven., sam. de 22h à l'aube, dim. de 15h à 19h30. Parcours de 18 trous : 2,59€. Selon météo.

GYMNASTIQUE :
Club sport et danse, Centre Jean-Verdier, 11, rue de Lancry.
Gym, stretching, claquette, yoga, classique.
ACSP .

B. Now scan the listings on pages 102 and 103 to find specific information.

1. At what time can you listen to a concert of music by Beethoven on June 27?

   _____

   _____

2. Where is there a concert by the Toronto Children's Chorus on June 26?

   _____

   _____

3. What are two American films showing in Paris?

   _____

   _____

4. Where can you take a dance class?

   _____

   _____

5. Where can you play miniature golf?

   _____

   _____

6. Where can you rent a canoe?

   _____

   _____

7. Where can you eat Spanish food?

   _____

   _____

8. Which two restaurants serve fondue?

   _____

   _____

Unité 7   *On fait les magasins.*

Leçon A

1 List several items of clothing that you might wear to each of the following places.

Modèle: au fast-food *un jean, une chemise, des chaussettes, des chaussures*

1. au cinéma _____

2. à la Martinique en été _____

3. en boîte _____

4. à Québec en hiver _____

5. au centre commercial _____

2 In English, state why you would go to each of the following places.

1. le centre commercial

_____

_____

2. le grand magasin

_____

_____

3. la teinturerie

_____

4. la cordonnerie

_____

5. le Quartier latin

_____

_____

6. le marché aux puces

_____

_____

3 The following people have next Monday off. Write a sentence telling what they are going to do, based on what they like.

Modèle: Ma sœur et moi, nous aimons les livres.
        Nous allons lire.

1. Tu aimes les hamburgers et les frites.

    _____

2. Elles aiment les desserts.

    _____

3. Vous aimez les sports.

    _____

4. Luc aime les boutiques.

    _____

5. J'aime Bach, Beethoven et Mozart.

    _____

6. Karine aime parler à ses amies.

    _____

7. Sandrine et Éric aiment faire du shopping.

    _____

8. Bruno et son amie aiment danser.

    _____

4 Fill in the blank with **à la**, **à l'**, **au** or **aux** to tell what the following people are giving to others.

Modèle: Je donne les livres ___*à l'*___ enfant.

1. Nous donnons les cahiers _____ professeur.

2. Henri donne un stylo _____ ingénieur.

3. La serveuse donne une pizza _____ garçons.

4. Elle donne une disquette _____ informaticien.

5. Vous donnez les jeux vidéo _____ cousin de Marc.

6. Tu donnes un cadeau _____ sœur de Christine?

7. Le prof donne les devoirs _____ élèves.

8. Marie et Sylvie donnent 15,24€ _____ coiffeur.

5 Write a complete sentence stating where certain people are doing various activities. Remember to use the correct form of the verb and **à la, à l', au** or **aux**.

Modèle:　je / regarder un film / le cinéma

　　　　Je regarde un film au cinéma.

1. Marc et Salim / faire les magasins / le centre commercial

　　　_____

　　　_____

2. je / chercher les tennis / les grands magasins

　　　_____

　　　_____

3. Élodie et Claire / chercher des pulls / la boutique

　　　_____

　　　_____

4. on / manger des crêpes / le café

　　　_____

　　　_____

5. tu / faire les devoirs / l'école

　　　_____

　　　_____

6. vous / manger un hamburger / le fast-food

　　　_____

　　　_____

7. ma mère / faire du shopping / le grand magasin

　　　_____

　　　_____

8. Laure / danser / la boum

　　　_____

　　　_____

Leçon B

---

6 | Write the opposite of each word or expression below.

1. grand _____

2. nouvelle _____

3. joli _____

4. courte _____

5. bon marché _____

6. moche _____

7. blanc _____

8. vieux _____

---

7 | Answer the following questions according to the **Enquête culturelle** in **Leçon B**.

1. What are the two largest French-speaking cities in the world?

_____

_____

2. Why is Montreal a good site for an underground city?

_____

_____

3. What can you find to do in Montreal's underground city?

_____

_____

4. How is everything in Montreal linked together underground?

_____

_____

5. Who imagined an underground city many centuries ago?

_____

6. Where do shopkeepers sometimes place sale items?

_____

_____

7. What does the sign **Soldes** mean in English?

_____

8 | Describe each item using the correct form of the adjective provided.

Modèle:

vieux
Les baskets sont vieilles.

1. blanc

_____

2. italien

_____

3. nouveau

_____

4. bon marché

_____

5. moche

_____

6. court

_____

7. gris

_____

8. vieux

_____

9. beau

_____

10. cher

_____

9 | Following the model, write two sentences to describe each picture. In each pair of sentences use two different adjectives from the following list.

petit / blanc / bon / joli / moche / cher / grand / beau / noir / nouveau / vieux

Modèle:

C'est une belle chemise.
C'est une chemise noire.

1. _____

_____

2. _____

_____

3. _____

_____

C'EST À TOI!
Level One

4. _____

_____

5. _____

_____

6. _____

_____

7. _____

_____

10 Write a new sentence each time by substituting the indicated word into the previous sentence and making any other necessary changes. Follow the models.

Modèles: Je préfère les beaux vêtements.

Ils *Ils préfèrent les beaux vêtements.*

cher *Ils préfèrent les vêtements chers.*

1. Nous _____

2. chemises _____

3. la _____

4. achetez _____

5. Tu _____

6. beau _____

7. Elle _____

8. anorak _____

9. J' _____

10. chaussettes _____

11. Ils _____

12. rouge _____

13. préfères _____

14. Il _____

15. jean _____

16. nouveau _____

17. Vous _____

18. chaussures _____

11

Find a match for each numbered word or expression. Write the letter of the correct choice next to the number.

A

_____ 1. rues piétonnes

_____ 2. les grands magasins

_____ 3. le marché aux puces

_____ 4. les fringues

_____ 5. faire du lèche-vitrines

_____ 6. une boutique

_____ 7. l'épicerie

_____ 8. les grandes surfaces

_____ 9. prêt-à-porter

_____ 10. les défilés

B

a. an outdoor market where secondhand clothes are sold

b. showings

c. ready-to-wear

d. huge supermarkets, discount stores

e. a small specialty shop

f. streets reserved for pedestrians only

g. to window-shop

h. cloth...

i. Galerie Lafayette, Printemps, Samaritaine

j. a store where one might buy snails or champagne

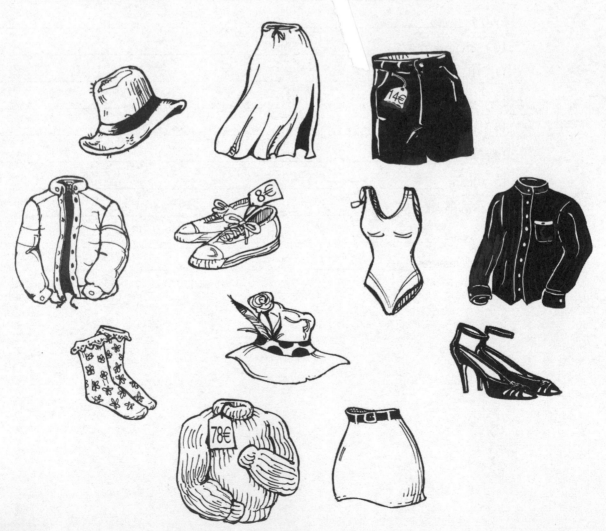

12 You are ordering some clothes from a French clothing catalogue for a female relative. She wears size 38. Use the catalogue descriptions to complete the order form on page 117. The first item of the order form has been filled in for you.

D   **Le maillot uni.** Décolleté arrondi devant et profond décolleté dos. Fond doublé. **En 80% polyamide, 20% élasthanne Lycra*.**

tailles	36	38	40	42	44	46
vert	60.6386	60.6396	60.6406	60.6416	60.6426	60.6436
marine	60.6506	60.6516	60.6526	60.6536	60.6546	60.6556
rouge	60.6446	60.6456	60.6466	60.6476	60.6486	60.6496
noir	60.6326	60.6336	60.6346	60.6346	60.6366	60.6376
prix			12,96€			

D   **Le bermuda-short.** Un prix extra! Monté sur ceinture plate devant, élastique dos. Devant, jeu de pinces piquées et lâchées de part et d'autre de la fermeture à glissière sous patte et bouton. Poches biais. Possibilité de rouler le bas et de le retenir par 1 patte pressionnée. En **toile 100% coton.**

tailles	36	38	40	42	44
blanc	98.5056	98.5066	98.5076	98.5086	98.5096
vert	36.8736	36.8746	36.8756	36.8766	36.8776
turquoise	98.4876	98.4986	98.4996	98.5006	98.5016
noir	98.5136	98.5146	98.5156	98.5166	98.5176
fuchsia	98.5216	98.5226	98.5236	98.5246	98.5256
beige	98.5296	98.5306	98.5316	98.5326	98.5336
prix			15,09€		

La jupe 2 longueurs. La forme droite pour être encore plus séduisante et élégante... votre ligne sera affinée, n'hésitez pas! Montée sur ceinture droite. 2 poches arrondies devant. Entièrement boutonnée au dos. Surpiqûres et boutons de coloris contrastés. Réalisée en **serge 100% coton.** 2 versions: longue ou courte.

La jupe courte. Longueur sous ceinture: 56 cm environ.

tailles	36	38	40	42
noir/blc	19.8456	19.8466	19.8476	19.8486
blc/marine	19.8386	19.8396	19.8406	19.816
prix		~~18,14€~~ 15,09€		

Le tee-shirt. Comment ne pas résister! Un tee-shirt pour moins de 13€ en **100% coton.** Pour cet été, vous pourrez le porter aisément et en plus il s'entretient facilement. Une **remise de 20%** vous attend! Encolure ronde dégagée avec un ravissant bord côtes imprimé fleurs. Emmanchures larges. Manches terminées par bord côtes imprimé. Ourlet à la base.

tailles	34/36	38/40	42/44	prix
blanc	12.9126	12.9136	12.9146	
vert	54.1796	54.1806	54.1816	
rose	54.1846	54.1856	54.1866	~~15,00€~~
jaune	54.1896	54.1906	54.1916	12,07€
noir	54.1946	54.1956	54.1966	

Le pantalon en toile. Très confortable pour l'été, en plus vous pouvez choisir dans notre large gamme de coloris. N'hésitez plus à ce prix! Élastique à la taille. 2 poches couture côtés. Entrejambe: 80 cm. Bas non terminés: 18 cm. En **100% coton.**

tailles	vert	turquoise	marine	rose	prix
34/36	62.7736	11.0806	94.1746	35.5546	
38/40	62.7756	11.0816	94.1766	35.5566	**12,18€**
42/44	62.7776	11.0826	94.1786	35.5586	
46/48	62.7796	11.0836	94.1806	35.5606	
50	62.7816	11.0846	94.2766	35.5626	**13,40€**
52	62.7826	11.0856	97.4316	35.5636	

Le pull torsade. De jolies torsades pour ce pull d'été plein d'allure. Ne résistez pas car son prix lui, vous fera craquer! Encolure ronde bordée par une torsade. Manches raglan. Maille fantaisie sur le devant. Finition par bord côtes. En **50% coton, 50% acrylique.**

tailles	34/36	38/40	42/44	46/48
mauve	52.7146	52.7156	52.7166	52.7176
ficelle	52.7066	52.7076	52.7086	52.7096
café	52.7106	52.7116	52.7126	52.7146
jaune	52.7186	52.7196	52.7206	52.7216
prix	**30,34€**	**31,86€**	**33,39€**	**34,91€**

Le jean multiplis. Toujours à la mode, le jean! Une coupe féminine pour un tout petit prix. Monté sur ceinture à passants. Fermeture à glissière, sous patte et bouton, encadrée de plis. Grandes et petites poches fantaisie devant. Pinces taille au dos. Poche à rabat boutonné. Entrejambes: 78 cm. Bas terminés: 18 cm. En **denim 100% coton.**

tailles	36	38	40	42
stone	70.6196	70.6206	70.6216	70.6226
prix		**24,24€**		**25,76€**
noir	70.6266	70.6276	70.6286	70.6296
prix		**26,68€**		**28,20€**
blanc	19.5616	19.5626	19.5636	19.5646
prix		**28,81€**		**30,34€**

A   La robe unie. Un **100% coton** et une forme pour vous avantager! Bustier sans manches. Découpes princesse devant et dos. Fermeture par boutons devant. Base évasée.

tailles	jaune	fuchsia	bleu	vert	prix
38	88.1446	88.1366	88.1606	88.1526	
40	88.1456	88.1376	88.1616	88.1536	**37,96€**
42	88.1466	88.1386	88.1626	88.1546	

B   L'ensemble sweat + mini-jupe. Ravissant! Et tellement confortable! Pour un prix... tout petit. **Le sweat:** encolure dégagée arrondie. Emmanchures carées. Fausse patte de boutonnage partant de la base. 1 poche gousset. Finition par bord côtes. **La jupe:** courte et droite montée sur ceinture élastique. Longueur sous ceinture: 45 cm. En **50% coton, 50% acrylique.**

tailles	34/36	38/40	42/44	46/48	prix
violet	63.4356	63.4366	63.4376	63.4386	
émeraude	69.8486	69.8496	69.8506	69.8516	**30,34€**
écru	69.8446	69.8456	69.8466	69.8476	

BON DE COMMANDE SUPPLÉMENTAIRE

à utiliser seulement si vous n'avez plus bon de commande étiqueté à votre nom et adresse.

Écrire en majuscules SVP
N° de cliente: |⎵|⎵|⎵|⎵|⎵|⎵|⎵| **920/132-920**

Nom ....
Prénom ....
Adresse ....
....
....
Localité ....
Code Postal |⎵|⎵|⎵|⎵|⎵|
Bureau distributeur ....

Si cette adresse est nouvelle, cochez cette case et indiquez votre ancienne adresse sur une feuille jointe. ☐

Désignation des articles	Numéro de référence	Quantité Nbre de lots	Prix unitaire	Montant Euros	Cts
1. *la robe bleue*	88.1606	1	37,96	37	96
2.					
3.					
4.					
5.					
6.					
7.					
8.					
9.					

1. a blue dress	6. a pair of green shorts
2. a pair of black jeans	7. a black and white skirt
3. a yellow sweater	8. a white T-shirt
4. a pair of pink pants	9. a purple sweatshirt and skirt outfit
5. a red bathing suit	

13 You want to buy some things for some friends at a **centre commercial** in France. You have a list with their American sizes. Rewrite the list in French in complete sentences and convert to French sizes. Use the chart on page 241 of your textbook.

Modèle: Julie / sweater / 14

Pour Julie je vais acheter un pull de taille 42.

1. Danièle / dress / 8

_____

_____

2. Steven / shirt / 16

_____

_____

3. Cathy / panty hose / 10

_____

_____

4. Mary / shirt / 12

_____

_____

5. Peter / sweater / 48

_____

_____

16 Read the following titles of ten articles in a French magazine. Write **F** next to the titles that state facts. Write **O** next to the titles that express opinions.

1. # La vie est belle   _____

2. *Élégance d'un style naturel*   _____

3. **Les vacances—pas chères**   _____

4. **L'Orchestre national de Lille visite Paris**   _____

5. *À prix imbattable:* trois maillots glamour   _____

6. **Animaux:** attirer les oiseaux dans son jardin   _____

7. *Desserts économiques*   _____

8. Brigitte Delmas, trois concerts à Paris   _____

9. **Sauces froides**   _____

10. *Testés pour vous:* les mascaras waterproof   _____

14 Replace the word or words in *italics* in each of the following sentences with a word borrowed from the French that means the same thing.

1. When I went to France last summer, I bought *a special cap that originated in the Pyrénées.* _____

2. I also bought some *pants made from a fabric that was first made in France.* _____

3. *That fabric* is used all over the world today for all kinds of clothes. _____

4. I bought those pants at a *small specialty store.* _____

5. The salesclerk told me I looked really *stylish* in those pants. _____

15 Fill in each blank with the correct present tense form of the verb **vendre**.

Modèle: Émile _____*vend*_____ des cahiers au magasin.

1. On _____ des hamburgers à Quick.

2. La vendeuse à la boutique _____ des maillots de bain.

3. Karine et moi, nous _____ des chaussures au centre commercial.

4. Je _____ des baskets aussi.

5. La FNAC _____ des tennis?

6. Vous _____ des pulls de taille 42?

7. Sophie et Marianne _____ des vestes.

8. Maurice, tu _____ des livres à ta boutique?

Unité 8   On fait les courses.

Leçon A

1 | Use the following illustrations to complete the crossword puzzle.

2 | Read the following statements and decide if they are true or false. If the statement is true, write **V** for **vrai**. If the statement is false, write **F** for **faux** and correct it.

_____   1. Une carotte est un légume.

_____

_____   2. La bouillabaisse est un dessert.

_____

_____   3. On a besoin d'une orange pour faire une bouillabaisse.

_____

_____   4. On mange une bouillabaisse au fast-food.

_____

_____   5. Les petits pois sont verts.

_____

_____   6. Une pomme de terre est un fruit.

_____

_____   7. On mange souvent un fruit après le repas.

_____

_____   8. Une crevette est un fruit.

_____

_____   9. Les crabes sont des légumes roses.

_____

3 Make a shopping list in English of things you need to buy to prepare fish soup from the recipe that follows. You already have these ingredients on hand: leeks (**poireaux**), fennel, thyme, bay leaves (**feuilles de laurier**), olive oil, saffron, garlic (**ail**), salt and pepper.

Soupe de poissons ★★

Pour 6 personnes. Préparation : 30 mn. Cuisson : 15 mn

- 2 kg de poissons mélangés : cabillaud, loup, baudroie...
- 250 g de crevettes cuites décortiquées
- 2 grosses tomates mûres
- 2 oignons rouges
- 2 blancs de poireaux
- 1 branche de fenouil
- 1 branche de thym
- 1 feuille de laurier
- 1 dl d'huile d'olive
- 6 pincées de safran
- 2 gousses d'ail
- sel, poivre

---

1. _____   3. _____

2. _____   4. _____

4 Match each French word or expression in Column A with its description in English in Column B. Write the letter of the description next to each number.

A	**B**
_____ 1. Marseille	a. a specialty of Strasbourg
_____ 2. le pâté de foie gras	b. the French national anthem
_____ 3. le bœuf bourguignon	c. a meat stew cooked in red wine
_____ 4. fort en vitamines	d. Marseille's main street
_____ 5. la "Marseillaise"	e. phrase written on food labels
_____ 6. le cassoulet	f. France's largest seaport
_____ 7. la Canebière	g. a soup made with crab, fish, tomatoes and onions
_____ 8. la bouillabaisse	h. a stew made with meat and white beans

5 | A. Use a form of the verb **vouloir** to tell what things the following people want.

Modèle: Je

Je veux un coca.

1. Ma sœur et moi, nous

_____

2. Chantal

_____

3. M. Bois et toi, vous

_____

4. Tu

_____

5. Gilles et Jean-Paul

_____

6. Jérôme

_____

B. Now tell what the following people want to do.

Modèle: Je

Je veux skier. _____

1. Éric et moi, nous

_____

2. Philippe et Denis

_____

3. Élise

_____

4. Tu

_____

5. Sophie et toi, vous

_____

6. Mon frère

_____

6 **A.** Now imagine that the people in Activity 5A can have what they want.

Modèle: *Je peux avoir un coca.*

1. _____
2. _____
3. _____
4. _____
5. _____
6. _____

B. Finally, imagine that the people in Activity 5B can do what they want.

Modèle: *Je peux skier.*

1. _____
2. _____
3. _____
4. _____
5. _____
6. _____

7 Use **ce, cet, cette** or **ces** to ask how much each of the following items costs.

Modèle: tomates *Combien coûtent ces tomates?*

1. poisson _____
2. crabe _____
3. crevettes _____
4. quiche _____
5. anorak _____
6. affiches _____
7. oignon _____
8. chien _____
9. haricots verts _____
10. eau minérale _____

8 | Categorize the following items according to the food groups to which they belong. Write each item in the appropriate column in the chart.

les oranges / les petits pois / les champignons / les pommes de terre / le jambon / le saucisson / les carottes / le lait / le bœuf / les oignons / le porc / le fromage / le yaourt / les haricots verts / le beurre / le pâté / le poulet

Fruits	Vegetables	Dairy	Meat
_____	_____	_____	_____
_____	_____	_____	_____
_____	_____	_____	_____
_____	_____	_____	_____
_____	_____	_____	_____
_____	_____	_____	_____

9 | To prepare an American cookout for your French host family, you will need various items. Next to each item write a sentence telling where you will go to buy it.

Modèle: une tarte aux fraises *On va à la pâtisserie.* _____

1. le ketchup _____
2. le bœuf _____
3. la moutarde _____
4. le pain _____
5. le fromage _____
6. le gâteau _____
7. les hot-dogs _____
8. les saucissons _____
9. le lait _____
10. le coca _____

10 | Answer the following questions according to the **Enquête culturelle** in **Leçon B**.

1. What does the expression **Repas sans pain, repas de rien** mean?

    _____

    _____

2. Why don't French bakeries wrap the **baguettes** they sell?

    _____

    _____

3. What do French schoolchildren often eat as a snack?

    _____

4. Other than pastry, what are three popular desserts in France?

    _____

    _____

5. What is the name of the province where many varieties of cheese are produced?

    _____

6. Have you ever eaten French cheese? If so, which kind(s)?

    _____

7. How do French teens get enough dairy products in their diets?

    _____

    _____

11 | Fill in the blanks using **de la, du, de l', des, le, la, l'** or **les**.

1. Tu n'aimes pas _____ café?

2.   Nous avons _____ pain.

3. Il y a _____ œufs là-bas.

4. Ma sœur aime _____ haricots verts.

5. Elle adore aussi _____ eau minérale.

6. Voici _____ légumes pour la soupe.

7. Nous mangeons _____ fruits après le repas.

8. Est-ce qu'il y a _____ pommes de terre?

9. Didier veut _____ fromage.

10. Anne préfère _____ hamburgers à Quick.

11. Patrick mange _____ soupe.

12. Maman aime _____ oignon dans l'omelette.

13. Vous aimez _____ tarte aux fraises, n'est-ce pas?

14. J'achète _____ moutarde.

15. Nous adorons _____ glace au chocolat.

---

12 To make each of the dishes below, state which ingredients you need to buy and which ones you don't need to buy.

Modèle: une quiche: oranges, œufs, fromage, oignon

Pour faire une quiche, j'achète des œufs, du fromage et de l'oignon. Je n'achète pas d'oranges.

1. une omelette: œufs, carottes, fromage, jambon, oignon

_____

_____

_____

2. une pizza: mayonnaise, fromage, champignons

_____

_____

_____

3. un sandwich: jambon, fromage, moutarde, yaourt, mayonnaise, pain

_____

_____

_____

4. une bouillabaisse: poissons, oignon, tomates, poulet

_____

_____

_____

13 Answer the questions that follow according to what you see in the pictures. Use each of the following expressions of quantity only once in your answers.

assez de / beaucoup de / un peu de / trop de / un morceau de / un pot de / trois boîtes de / une bouteille de / un kilo de

Modèle: Combien de croissants est-ce qu'il y a?
Il y a beaucoup de croissants.

1. Combien d'oranges est-ce qu'il y a?

   _____

2. Combien de petits pois est-ce qu'il y a?

   _____

3. Combien de coca est-ce qu'il y a?

   _____

4. Combien de confiture est-ce qu'il y a?

   _____

 5.   Combien de fromage est-ce qu'il y a?

_____

 6.   Combien de gâteau est-ce qu'il y a?

_____

 7.   Combien de lait est-ce qu'il y a?

_____

 8.   Combien de champignons est-ce qu'il y a?

_____

14 | Answer the following questions about food shopping in France and in the French-speaking world. Place the letter of the best answer from Column B in the blank next to each number in Column A.

A	B
_____ 1. When do open-air markets open?	a. It offers individualized service.
_____ 2. For what reasons might customers be attracted to the open-air market?	b. It's a shopping basket.
	c. One is a convenient corner grocery store, the other is larger and sells a variety of products under one roof.
_____ 3. What is a **sac à provisions**?	
_____ 4. What products might be sold at open-air markets in Guadeloupe or Martinique?	d. You can buy most meat products.
	e. They open early in the morning.
_____ 5. What is one advantage of a family-owned specialty shop?	f. You can buy prepared salads and cold meat dishes.
_____ 6. What is the difference between a **boulangerie** and a **pâtisserie**?	g. They might sell tuna, lobster, clams, bananas, papayas, mangoes, avocados, guavas and yams.
_____ 7. What can you buy at a **boucherie**?	h. Busy lifestyles limit the time spent on meal preparation.
_____ 8. What can you buy at a **charcuterie**?	i. You can buy it at the **boucherie chevaline**.
_____ 9. Where can you buy horse meat?	j. One sells bread and rolls, the other pastries, cakes, pies and cookies.
_____ 10. What is the difference between an **épicerie** and a **supermarché**?	k. It offers the freshest food, reasonable prices, regional specialties and seasonal foods.
_____ 11. Why are **les produits surgelés** becoming more popular in France?	

Leçon C

15 Look at this list of the best fruits and vegetables to buy at French open-air markets in July and August.

LE MARCHÉ DE JUILLET

LES LÉGUMES
Arrivée des haricots à écosser, des blettes, des endives d'été. C'est la pleine période des haricots verts, des fèves, de l'oseille, des salades d'été, du concombre, des herbes aromatiques.

LES FRUITS
Abricots, pêches, prunes et poires guyot font une entrée très remarquée. Sont également présentes les framboises, les fraises, les nectarines, les melons, les cerises. Mangeons-les avec délice, crus, en compotes, en tartes ou conservons-les pour l'hiver.

LE MARCHÉ D'AOÛT

LES LÉGUMES
C'est l'abondance : aubergines, tomates, courgettes, poivrons, piments, artichauts, céleris, choux-fleurs, salades... Pensons à faire des conserves de cornichons.

LES FRUITS
Le choix est vaste avec les prunes, les pêches, les abricots, les poires d'été, les melons, les pastèques. En fin de mois, saluons l'arrivée du raisin.

Underline the illustrations of items to buy in July and circle the ones to buy in August.

16 | Answer the following questions according to the **Enquête culturelle** in **Leçon C**.

1. Where is Guadeloupe located?

   _____

2. What are some of the main products of Guadeloupe?

   _____

3. Is it possible to bargain with the merchants at open-air markets in Guadeloupe?

   _____

   _____

4. What is responsible for variations in fruit prices?

   _____

5. How many U.S. pounds are in one kilogram?

   _____

6. How many U.S. pounds are in 500 grams?

   _____

17 | Use **plus**, **moins** or **aussi** to compare an item in Column A to an item in Column C, using the appropriate form of an adjective in Column B. Compare one fruit to another fruit and vegetables to other vegetables.

A	B	C
1. une pomme	mûr	une fraise
2. un raisin	petit	une poire
3. une pêche	rouge	une pastèque
4. une cerise	beau	une orange
5. une banane	cher	un melon
6. les haricots verts	vert	les petits pois
7. les pommes de terre	grand	les carottes
8. les tomates		les oignons rouges
9. les champignons		les oignons blancs

Modèles: *Une pomme est plus rouge qu'une orange.*

Les pommes de terre sont moins chères que les petits pois.

1. _____

2. _____

3. _____

4. _____

5. _____

6. _____

7. _____

8. _____

9. _____

18 | Think in French as you read the following recipe three times. Then answer the questions.

SALADE DE FRUITS PARISIENNE

20 min

PRÉPARATION : 20 minutes
POUR 4 PERSONNES

● 1 grappe de raisin blanc ● 1 grappe de raisin noir ● 20 fraises ● quelques myrtilles ● 1 poire ● 1/2 mangue ● 2 kiwis ● 1 banane ● 1/2 litre de glace à la fraise ● 3 dl de coulis de framboises ● 1 citron ● quelques feuilles de menthe fraîche.

Laver et éplucher les fruits, détailler (avec des ciseaux) les grappes de raisins en grappillons de 4 à 5 grains. Couper les gros fruits en tranches minces puis les arroser de jus de citron. Placer au centre des assiettes deux boules de glace puis, au fond, verser un lit de coulis de framboises. Ensuite, disposer les fruits en couronne en formant des taches de couleur harmonieuses et décorer de feuilles de menthe fraîche.

1. From what city in France does this recipe originate?

   _____

2. How long does it take to make this salad?

   _____

3. How many people will this recipe serve?

   _____

4. What color grapes are needed?

_____

_____

5. What are some other fruits needed for this recipe?

_____

_____

_____

6. After the fruits are washed and peeled, how do you cut the larger fruits?

_____

_____

7. What kind of ice cream do you need?

_____

_____

8. How many scoops of ice cream should you put on the center of each plate?

_____

_____

9. Would you serve this salad during the meal or after the meal? Why?

_____

_____

Unité 9 À *la maison*

Leçon A

1 List each of the pieces of furniture and appliances under the name of the room where you are most likely to find it. If an item is commonly found in more than one room, you may list it under each one.

un canapé / un lit / un four / une table / une lampe / un bureau / un fauteuil / une cuisinière / un micro-onde / une armoire / une stéréo / un frigo

Le séjour	La cuisine	La chambre
_____	_____	_____
_____	_____	_____
_____	_____	_____
_____	_____	_____
_____	_____	_____

2 Make a list of eight common household items by combining the groups of letters. You will need to use at least two groups to name each item and you may need to use as many as four. Use each group of letters only once.

toi	can	bur	sté	gno
réo	bai	dou	cha	apé
ise	mag	let	eau	nét
osc	che	tes	ope	ire

1. _____   5. _____

2. _____   6. _____

3. _____   7. _____

4. _____   8. _____

3 You are trying to decide where to stay in France. Read the following hotel descriptions and then fill out the chart on page 139 to compare their features. First, write how many rooms are available in each hotel. Then put a check next to each item mentioned in each hotel's description.

GAUTHIER

À mi-chemin entre Montmartre et l'Arc de Triomphe, l'hôtel GAUTHIER vous donne le meilleur de PARIS. Des liaisons rapides au cœur de la capitale par le métro et l'autobus, un accès facile en voiture, à proximité du périphérique.

Le Plus Grand Hôtel 2 Étoiles d'Europe

Avec 648 chambres l'hôtel GAUTHIER est aujourd'hui le plus grand deux étoiles d'Europe. Chaque chambre, équipée de deux lits individu-els ou d'un grand lit, dispose d'une salle de bains, de toilettes, d'un téléphone direct, d'une télévision, (15 chaînes françaises et étrangères), d'une radio, d'un réveil automatique et d'un minitel dans 200 chambres.

À votre service trois restaurants, un bar-terrasse, un salon et des salles de réunions mais aussi des boutiques, un comptoir de réservations spectacles/excursions et un immense parking gardé.

VICTORIA

Mer bleue, plage bordée de palmiers, végétation luxuriante, est aujourd'hui encore le symbole de la Côte d'Azur, du faste et du rêve. Fréquentée autrefois par les têtes couronnées, la station a su conserver le luxe et la féérie des années 30.

Situé en plein cœur de ville, proche des plages, du tennis et du Casino, l'hôtel VICTORIA profite d'une vue imprenable sur la mer et la montagne.

Un Grand Hôtel de la Belle Époque

L'hôtel VICTORIA a gardé tout son cachet Belle Époque. Il offre 80 chambres confortables avec salle de bains ou douche/toilettes, téléphone. En pension complète ou en demi-pension, ses trois salles de restaurant vous permettront de découvrir une cuisine soignée. L'hôtel met également à votre disposition deux salons et un bar.

LA VARENNE

LA VARENNE est à l'est de Paris, à deux pas d'un important centre d'affaires et d'activités, non loin du complexe DISNEYLAND PARIS à 13 km à peine de la capitale.

Travail, Détente et Confort

L'hôtel LA VARENNE accueillera sa clientèle dans 85 chambres confortables avec salle de bains/toilettes, téléphone, télévision. Certaines chambres seront dotées d'un coin cuisine équipé.

L'hôtel comprendra également un restaurant pour les séjours en pension complète et en demi-pension, une brasserie, une salle de remise en forme avec sauna, trois salles modulables (de 50 à 150 m²) pour les congrès et séminaires et un vaste parking.

	Gauthier	Victoria	La Varenne
Nombres de chambres			
Choix de deux lits individuels ou d'un grand lit			
Salle de bains			
W.-C./Toilettes			
Téléphone			
Télévision			
Radio			
Restaurants dans l'hôtel			
Boutiques dans l'hôtel			
Douches			

4 | Match each French expression in Column A with the correct description in English in Column B. Write the letter corresponding to your choice in the blank next to the number.

	A		B
_____	1. le centre-ville	a.	the room with a bathtub, a sink, a bidet and a vanity
_____	2. la banlieue	b.	what the interior of an apartment building often overlooks
_____	3. une cour	c.	the suburbs
_____	4. une armoire	d.	generally, the most expensive area of a city in which to live
_____	5. la salle de bains	e.	the room with the toilet
_____	6. les W.-C./les toilettes	f.	a piece of furniture used to store clothing
_____	7. un bidet	g.	what the French use instead of a washcloth
_____	8. un gant de toilette	h.	a bathroom fixture used for personal hygiene

5 | **A.** Draw a line connecting each item in Column A to the place in Column B where the item is most likely to be found. Use each item and location only once.

               A   B

1. les légumes frais   a. sur le bureau

2. les beaux canapés   b. dans le salon

3. les dictionnaires français   c. dans la chambre

4. les chaussettes brunes   d. dans le frigo

5. les jolis tapis   e. sous les tables

6. les grands lits   f. dans l'armoire

7. les nouvelles baignoires   g. dans le four

8. les petites boîtes de légumes   h. dans les salles de bains

9. les tartes chaudes   i. dans le placard

B. According to the lines you have drawn in Part A, write a sentence for each item that indicates where it is likely to be found. The first two sentences have been done for you.

1. *Il y a des légumes frais dans le frigo.*

2. *Il y a de beaux canapés dans le salon.*

3. _____

4. _____

5. _____

6. _____

7. _____

8. _____

9. _____

6 | **A.** In the following picture, label the different parts of the house and all of the items near it, using the choices below.

le premier étage / les fleurs / l'arbre / le rez-de-chaussée / la chambre /
le jardin / le grenier / la voiture / la cuisine / le garage / la salle à manger /
le salon / l'escalier / le sous-sol

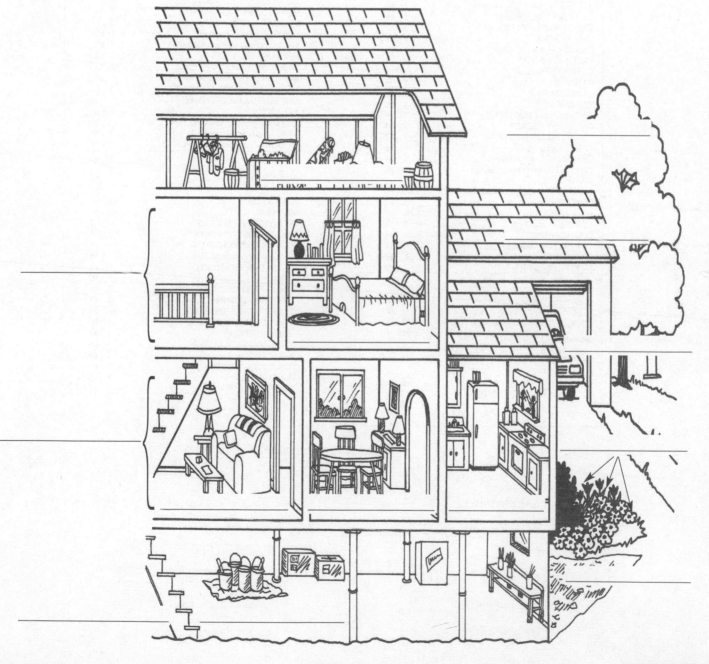

B. David, Raoul, Nathalie and Caroline are shopping at BHV, a department store in Paris. Using the store directory below, locate the floor and the department where each person will find the items he or she is looking for. Then write the location on the line next to each item.

BHV — RIVOLI

BACS ET POTS	s/s	c2
BAGAGES	2	c3
BALANCES/PÈSE PERSONNE	3	c5
BÂTIMENT (matériaux)	4	c1
BIJOUTERIE	rdc	b1
BLANC	2	b4
BOIS (détail/coupé)	4	d1
BUREAU (accessoires/classement)	1	b5
CADRES/ENCADREMENT	5	c6
CAFETIÈRES ÉLECTRIQUES	3	c2
CALCULATRICES	1	b6
CAMÉRAS/CAMÉSCOPES	1	d1
CAMPING (fév./oct.)	2	a2
CAMPING (nov./janv.)	s/s	c2
CANAPÉS	5	c4
CARRELAGES	4	b3
CARTABLES	1	b6
CASSEROLES/COCOTTES...	3	c4
CASSETTES VIERGES	1	b1
CASSETTES ENREGISTRÉES	1	a3
CAVE (articles de)	s/s	a6
CHAMBRES (meubles/literie)	6	b3
CHASSE (équipement/vêtements)	1	c6
CHAUFFAGE	s/s	a1
CHEMISES HOMME	rdc	b5
CLIMATISEURS	3	b2
COLLANTS/BAS	rdc	d1
CONGÉLATEURS	3	a1
COUTELLERIE	3	c4
COUVERTURES/COUETTES...	6	a4
CRAVATES/ÉCHARPES	rdc	b6
CUISINE (articles de)	3	c3
FAÏENCE	3	b5
FAUTEUILS	5	c4
FERS À REPASSER	3	c2
FLEURS ARTIFICIELLES	2	c3
FOURS/FOURS MICRO-ONDES	3	b3
LAMPES ET LAMPADAIRES	2	c5
LAVE-LINGE	3	b2
LAVE-VAISSELLE	3	b2
LINGE DE MAISON	2	b4
LINGERIE FÉMININE	rdc	c2
LISTES MARIAGE/CADEAUX	3	a6
LIVRES/B.D.	1	b4
LUSTRERIE	2	c5

MACHINES (à coudre/à tricoter)	3	b3
MACHINES À REPASSER	3	b3
MAGNÉTOSCOPES	1	a2
MAROQUINERIE	rdc	b4
MATELAS/SOMMIERS	6	b4
MÉNAGE (articles de)	3	c4
MERCERIE	2	d1
MEUBLES BUREAU (adulte)	5	b1
MEUBLES BUREAU (junior)	6	a2
MEUBLES DE CUISINE	3	b6
MEUBLES DE JARDIN(fév./oct.)	2	b2
MEUBLES DE JARDIN(nov./janv.)	s/s	c2
MEUBLES DE SALLE DE BAINS	2	b6
MEUBLES EN KIT	4	c2
MEUBLES EN KIT (sept/oct.)	2	b2
MEUBLES (séjour/environnement)	5	b3
MEZZANINES	5	a3
MICRO INFORMATIQUE/VIDÉO	1	d3
MIROITERIE DE SALLE DE BAINS	2	b5
MIROITERIE D'AMEUBLEMENT	5	c1
MODELISME/MAQUETTISME	1	d3
MOQUETTE	6	d2
MOTO (accessoires/vêtements)	s/s	d6
MOUSSE (plaques/découpé)	4	d6
MUSIQUE (instruments/partitions)	1	b1
SACS À DOS	1	c5
SACS À MAINS	rdc	b4
SALLE DE BAINS (accessoires)	2	b5
SÈCHE-LINGE	3	b1
SERRURERIE	s/s	b4
SOUDURE	s/s	d4
SOUS-VÊTEMENTS DAME	rc	c2
SOUS-VÊTEMENTS ENFANTS	1	c3
SOUS-VÊTEMENTS HOMME	rc	a4
SPORT (vêtements/matériel)	1	c4
STORES (intérieur/extérieur)	4	d4
STYLOS	1	b5
TABLEAUX/REPRODUCTIONS	5	c6
TAPIS/TAPIS D'ORIENT	6	c2
TÉLÉPHONES/RÉPONDEURS	s/s	a3
TÉLÉPHONES/RÉPONDEURS	1	b5
TÉLÉVISION/VIDÉO	1	a2
TISSUS D'AMEUBLEMENT	4	c4
TOILES CIRÉES	2	a3
TONDEUSES À GAZON	s/s	c2
TRAVAUX PHOTO	1	d2
TRINGLES À RIDEAUX	4	d3

David cherche:

1. des stylos et des crayons. _____

2. une chemise. _____

3. des vêtements de ski. _____

Raoul cherche:

1. une lampe pour sa chambre. _____

2. une télévision. _____

3. un bon livre. _____

Nathalie cherche:

1. un micro-onde. _____

2. des fleurs artificielles pour le salon. _____

Caroline cherche:

1. un sac à dos. _____

2. un magnétoscope. _____

3. des bas. _____

7 Draw a line between each statement or question in Column A and a logical response in Column B.

A

1. Je vous présente mon frère, Roger. Roger, Philippe.

2. Voici des fleurs, Madame.

3. Vous voulez un jus de fruit?

4. Bonsoir, Monsieur.

5. Où est votre voiture?

6. Ces fleurs sont très jolies.

B

a. Bonsoir, Madame.

b. Elle est dans le garage.

c. Enchanté.

d. Oui, je veux bien.

e. Elles viennent du jardin.

f. Que vous êtes gentil!

8 Chantal is going to have dinner with her mother's friends, Charles and Claire Dupont, whom she has never met before. Write the probable conversation between the people shown in each frame on the lines below the picture. Use the caption above the picture as a guide to what is happening.

2. Mme Dupont greets Chantal, welcomes her and introduces Chantal to her husband.

1. Chantal greets Mme Dupont.

_____

_____

_____

3. Chantal responds to the introduction, greets M. Dupont and gives flowers to Mme Dupont.

4. Mme Dupont thanks Chantal and tells her husband to take the flowers. Mme Dupont tells him that the blue vase is on the table in the kitchen.

_____

_____

_____

5. M. Dupont invites everyone into the living room.

6. Mme Dupont asks Chantal if she would like some mineral water. Chantal accepts.

_____

_____

_____

9 Answer the following questions according to the **Enquête culturelle** in **Leçon B**.

1. How would you describe a typical house in Normandy?

   _____

   _____

2. What does a typical house in the south of France look like?

   _____

   _____

3. What are two distinctive styles of French houses? Where do you find each one?

   _____

   _____

4. How does **le premier étage** in a French-speaking country differ from "the first floor" in the United States?

   _____

   _____

   _____

5. Where do most French families have a vacation home? Where else might they spend their vacation?

   _____

   _____

   _____

6. In France, what gift do dinner guests usually bring to their hosts?

   _____

7. How is the term **les apéros** used in French-speaking countries?

   _____

   _____

---

10 | Using the pictures, write complete sentences telling what the following people are having to eat or drink.

Modèle: Je

Je prends des pommes.

1. Tu

_____

2. Charles et moi, nous

_____

3. Karine

_____

4. Les garçons

    _____

5. Mon père

    _____

6. Vous

    _____

7. Annick et Laure

    _____

11 Complete the brochure for **La Vitalé** Health Spa by writing a caption for each picture below. Use imperative verb forms to tell people what they can do there.

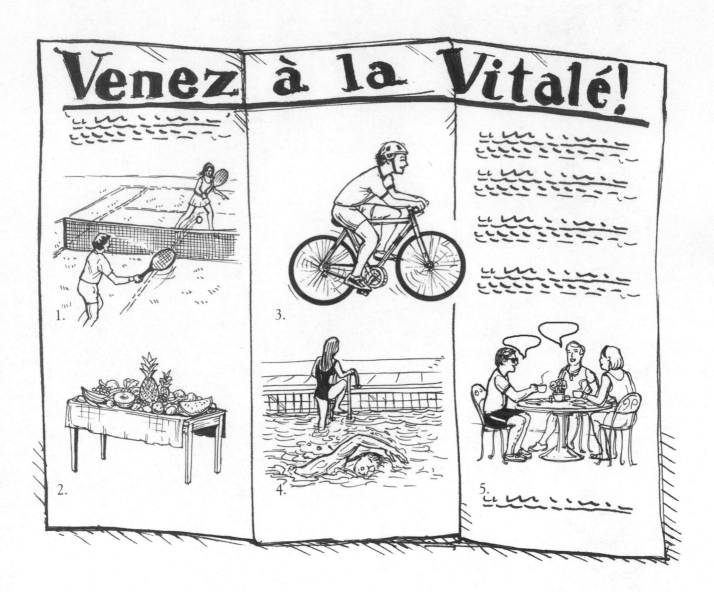

1. _____

2. _____

3. _____

4. _____

5. _____

12 | You are babysitting for a child who misbehaves. According to what he says, tell him what to do or what not to do.

Modèles: Je ne veux pas manger ces légumes. *Mange ces légumes!*

         Je veux téléphoner à mon ami au Japon. *Ne téléphone pas à ton ami au Japon!*

1. Je ne veux pas faire mes devoirs. _____

2. Je ne veux pas porter mon manteau. _____

3. Je veux regarder la télé. _____

4. Je veux manger deux desserts. _____

5. Je veux prendre trois cocas. _____

6. Je ne veux pas parler à ma grand-mère. _____

13 | Write complete sentences to suggest activities that you and your friends can do this weekend.

Modèle: *Allons au centre commercial.* _____

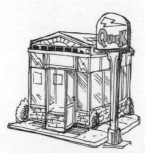

1. _____

2. _____

3. _____

4. _____

5. _____

6. _____

7. _____

8. _____

14 **A.** Rewrite each group of items in the order in which they are eaten in France.

1. le goûter, le déjeuner, le dîner, le petit déjeuner

   _____

2. la salade, le café, le dessert, le fromage, l'entrée, les hors-d'œuvre, le plat principal

   _____

   _____

B. Bob is staying with a family in France. He wants to impress the family with his good table manners and so he has made some resolutions. Read Bob's resolutions and then advise him in English how to behave more appropriately to impress his French hosts.

1. I will not put my elbows on the table and I will keep one hand in my lap.

   _____

   _____

2. I will cut my meat all at one time.

   _____

   _____

3. After I cut my meat, I will put my silverware on my plate and then pick up the fork in my right hand and continue eating.

   _____

   _____

   _____

4. I will eat my vegetables with a spoon.

   _____

   _____

5. I will slice my bread with a knife.

   _____

   _____

6. I will put my silverware next to my plate when I have finished eating.

   _____

   _____

15 | A. Compare these formal place settings from France, England and the United States. Then put a check in each column of the chart to which the statement applies.

France

Angleterre

États-Unis

1. Assiette et serviette
2. Couteau de table
3. Couteau à poisson
4. Cuiller à soupe
5. Fourchette à melon
6. Fourchette de table
7. Fourchette à poisson
8. Fourchette supplémentaire
9. Couteau à dessert
10. Cuiller à dessert
11. Fourchette à dessert
12. Couteau à beurre
13. Beurrier individuel
14. Verre à eau
15. Coupe de champagne

	France	Angleterre	États-Unis
1. La serviette est sur l'assiette.			
2. La fourchette à melon est à droite de la cuiller à soupe.			
3. Il n'y a pas de fourchette à melon.			
4. Le couteau à dessert est au-dessus de la fourchette à dessert.			
5. Il y a cinq fourchettes.			
6. Il n'y a pas de couteau à dessert.			
7. La fourchette à poisson est à gauche de la fourchette de table.			
8. Le couteau à beurre est sur le beurrier individuel.			
9. La coupe de champagne est à gauche du verre à eau.			
10. La cuiller à soupe est à droite du couteau à poisson.			
11. La fourchette supplémentaire est à gauche de l'assiette.			

B. Rewrite the following sentences, making all necessary changes to correct them.

1. On prend le petit déjeuner à 4h30. _____

2. Le couteau est à gauche de la serviette. _____

3. La soupe est dans le verre. _____

4. Le sel et le poivre sont dans un bol. _____

5. On prend le goûter le matin. _____

6. La fourchette est au-dessus de l'assiette. _____

7. On mange une salade avec une nappe. _____

8. Le dîner est à midi. _____

---

16 Answer the following questions according to the **Enquête culturelle** in **Leçon C**.

1. What three North African countries form **le Maghreb**?

   _____

2. What two bodies of water border Morocco?

   _____

3. What is the capital of Morocco?

   _____

4. What languages are spoken in Morocco?

   _____

5. What is Ramadan?

   _____

6. How do Muslims celebrate the end of Ramadan?

   _____

7. What do young people do in the afternoon of **l'Aïd el-Fitr**?

   _____

   _____

8. What is the national drink of Morocco?

   _____

17 | Write sentences telling where people put their things by using a form of **mettre** and a logical choice from the following list.

dans le garage / dans le frigo / dans la cuisine / dans la chambre / sur la table / dans le séjour / avec le magnétoscope

Modèle: Je / les fleurs
Je mets les fleurs sur la table.

1.   Mon père / la voiture

_____

2.   Daniel et moi, nous / le four

_____

3.   Vous / la stéréo

_____

4.   Sandrine et Pierre / le lit

_____

5.   Antoine / le lait

_____

6.   Tu / les vidéocassettes

_____

18 | Read the ads for home appliances. Using contextual clues, identify in English each appliance advertised, give its price (if it is mentioned) and name at least two features that make the appliance unique.

Assistance technique
Ce micro-ondes, équipé d'un gril, enchaîne toutes les opérations depuis la décongélation au maintien au chaud, en passant par la cuisson et le gril. Capacité: 24 litres. Une touche « Quick » mémorise un temps de cuisson de 1 à 180 secondes. Programmation 24 heures à l'avance. Livré avec plateau tournant et livre de recettes. Micro-ondes 2745 AG de Moulinex (518,33€).

1._____

_____

_____

C'EST À TOI!
Level One

Noir design

Sobriété des lignes pour cette machine à express équipée d'une pompe électro-magnétique de 15 bars. Elle garantit un café mousseux quelles que soient la quantité de mouture et la granulométrie. Un filtre unique sert pour réaliser une ou deux tasses. Réservoir amovible. Couleur : bronze. Equipée d'un distributeur de vapeur pour faire un vrai cappuccino. Grancafé de Seb (167,69€).

2. _____

_____

_____

Activités multiples occupation réduite

Cet appareil regroupe une plaque de cuisson (tout gaz, mixte ou électrique), un four à convection naturelle de 35 litres avec gril et tournebroche, et un lave-vaisselle 6 couverts à 7 programmes. Dimensions : H : 85 cm ; P : 60 cm ; L : 60 cm. Trio de Candy (de 943,66€ à 1 019,88€ selon la table).

3. _____

_____

_____

Unité 10   *La santé*

1 | Using the numbered parts of the body in the picture, fill in the crossword puzzle that follows.

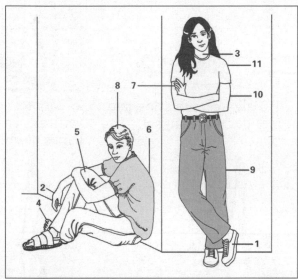

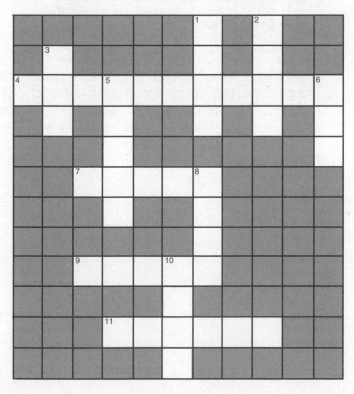

2 Scan the description of the fitness exercise that follows. Find the names of at least four different body parts and write them below.

La chandelle

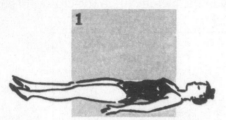

1) S'allonger sur le dos, paumes des mains au sol.

2) Monter les jambes à la verticale en marquant un temps d'arrêt à 30° et à 60°.

3) Lorsque les jambes sont à angle droit, respirer profondément. En prenant appui sur les mains, soulever les fesses, puis le dos jusqu'à ce que le corps repose sur les épaules et la nuque.

4) Les mains soutenant le corps, garder cette position aussi longtemps que l'on se sent à l'aise.

_____   _____

_____   _____

_____

3 Answer the following questions according to the **Enquête culturelle** in **Leçon A**.

1. Where is Chamonix located? What is Chamonix famous for?

_____

_____

2. What is the French word for the means of transportation that skiers and tourists use to get to the top of a mountain?

_____

_____

3. What is the name of the highest mountain in **les Alpes**? How did it get its name?

_____

_____

4. When do French students have winter vacation? How long does it last?

_____

_____

5. What are **les classes de neige**?

_____

_____

6. Which sport is more popular among French teens: downhill skiing or cross-country skiing?

_____

_____

7. What is the French equivalent of the proverb "Cold hands, warm heart"?

_____

_____

4 | **A.** List each of the activities that follow under the appropriate heading. Base your decisions on whether the activity promotes or jeopardizes good health.

manger de la salade / regarder la télé / faire du sport / prendre du coca / manger de la glace / jouer au tennis / prendre de l'eau / manger des frites / manger des fruits / être paresseux

Bon pour la santé	**Mauvais pour la santé**
_____	_____
_____	_____
_____	_____
_____	_____

B. Now, using your lists from Activity 4A, write four complete sentences suggesting steps to follow and things to avoid in order to maintain good health. In each of your recommendations, use the expressions **il faut** and **il ne faut pas** and include one item from each list: **Bon pour la santé** and **Mauvais pour la santé**. As you select items from the lists, make sure that your choices are logical pairs.

Modèle: *Il faut manger des fruits, mais il ne faut pas manger de la glace.*

1. _____

_____

2. _____

_____

3. _____

_____

4. _____

_____

Leçon B

5 **A.** Draw a line from each question in Column A to the best answer in Column B.

A	B

1. Tu attends Georges et Paul?   a. Non, je n'achète rien.

2. Tu vas à la boum?   b. Non, je n'étudie plus l'espagnol.

3. Tu achètes un cadeau?   c. Non, je ne vais pas à la boum.

4. Tu vas souvent à Paris?   d. Non, je n'attends personne.

5. Tu étudies toujours l'espagnol?   e. Non, je ne vais jamais à Paris.

B. What parts of the body do you use to do the following activities?

Modèle: skier *les jambes, les pieds, les bras, les mains, les yeux, les genoux*

1. faire les devoirs _____

2. faire du vélo _____

3. regarder la télé _____

4. jouer au foot _____

5. jouer au tennis _____

6. manger des frites _____

7. téléphoner _____

6 How would you . . .

1.　say that you want an appointment with the doctor?

_____

_____

2.　say that you have a toothache?

_____

_____

3.　say that you want an appointment as soon as possible?

_____

_____

4.　ask if the doctor is there this afternoon?

_____

_____

5.　say that you can't come tomorrow morning?

_____

_____

6.　say that you can come tomorrow afternoon at 2:30 P.M.?

_____

_____

7 | Answer the following questions according to the **Enquête culturelle** in **Leçon B**.

1. What two major Swiss cities are located on Lake Geneva?

_____

_____

2. What is the French name for Lake Geneva?

_____

_____

3. What three international organizations have their main offices in Geneva?

_____

_____

4. What percentage of Swiss people speak French?

_____

_____

5. In addition to French, what other languages do the Swiss speak?

_____

_____

6. In the dialogue, the dentist's family name is Odermatt. What part of Switzerland do you think his family originally came from?

_____

_____

7. For what two products is Switzerland famous?

_____

_____

8 Tell about yourself by completing each sentence with an infinitive or an infinitive expression. You may choose from the following list or use any other infinitives or infinitive expressions that you know.

danser / lire / sortir / dormir / étudier / manger / skier / faire les courses / jouer au tennis / travailler / téléphoner à des ami(e)s

1. J'adore _____ le samedi matin.

2. J'aime _____ le samedi soir.

3. Demain je vais _____.

4. Je désire _____.

5. Il faut _____.

6. Je n'aime pas _____.

7. Je préfère _____.

8. Je ne vais pas _____.

9. Je veux _____ après les cours.

9 In a complete sentence, tell how frequently you engage in the following activities: never, not anymore, often or always.

Modèle: aller au cinéma avec mes parents

Je ne vais jamais au cinéma avec mes parents. or

Je ne vais plus au cinéma avec mes parents. or

Je vais souvent au cinéma avec mes parents. or

Je vais toujours au cinéma avec mes parents.

1. écouter de la musique

   _____

2. faire les devoirs après les cours

   _____

3. étudier la géographie

   _____

4. skier

   _____

5. aller au centre commercial

   _____

6. jouer aux jeux vidéo

   _____

7. prendre le petit déjeuner

_____

8. jouer au basket avec mes amis à minuit

_____

9. nager

_____

10. téléphoner à ma grand-mère

_____

_____

---

10 | Disagree with the following statements by writing the opposite of each one.

Modèle: Il y a quelqu'un dans la voiture.

Il n'y a personne dans la voiture.
_____

1. Tu manges quelque chose.

_____

2. Ma famille et moi, nous allons souvent en vacances.

_____

_____

3. Ta sœur et toi, vous prenez souvent des croissants.

_____

_____

4. Je fais toujours du roller.

_____

_____

5. Joseph n'écoute personne.

_____

6. Martine et Véronique ne cherchent rien.

_____

_____

7. Je ne joue plus au tennis.

_____

8. Salim achète des poissons rouges.

_____

Leçon C

12 │ For each medical problem in this activity, circle the name of the most appropriate medical professional or facility to visit for treatment. For help in making your decision, refer to the following directory.

———— SERVICE DE SANTÉ ————

• MÉDECINS GÉNÉRALISTES - SPÉCIALISTES

ALLEMAND J.-L. - 10, Avenue Roger Varrey
CHARVOLIN J.-P. - 1, Quai de la Butte
DELATTRE P. - 3, Place de l'Hôtel de Ville (Général Valet)
EL AHL N. - 26, Quai du Général Leclerc
JEANDOT N. - 8, Rue de la Commanderie
LAURENCE G. - 5, Avenue du Capitaine Tulasne
MEDJIAN Brigitte - 1, Faubourg Saint-Jacques
COMOY P. - (Anest.-Réa.) - 30, Rue du Chevalier d'Albizzi
MARGUERITTE A. - (App. Digestif) - 15, Quai Ragobert
VIEL J. - (Cardiologie) - 35, Avenue Roger Varrey
MÉNAGE C. - (Chirurgie) - 8, Avenue Gambetta
MERCIER A. - (Chirurgie) - 8, Avenue Gambetta
MERCIER J.-F. - (Chirurgie) - 5, Avenue Gambetta
BARET Mireille - (Dermato.-Vénéro.) - 6, Rue Basse-Pêcherie
MORANGE C. - (Gynécologie) - 13, Rue Voltaire
FLEURY B. - (Méd. du Travail) - 2, Quai de la Butte
ROUAT D. - (Ophtalmologie) - 26, Quai du Général Leclerc
VOUTERS H. - (Ophtalmologie) - 37, Rue Aristide Briand
CARRÉ D. - (Oto-Rhino-Laryngologie) - 7, Rue Pasteur
APARICIO M. - (Pédiatrie) - 1, Rue des Vignes Saint-Jacques
CORBIN Marie-Agnès - (Psychiatrie) - 2, Avenue de Mayen
ROSSIGNEUX M. - (Radiologie) - 33, Quai Général Leclerc
BOLUSSET M. - (Stomatologie) - 2, Place Saint-Thibault

• CHIRURGIENS - DENTISTES

ALLEMAND Anne-Marie - 10, Avenue Roger Varrey
BIGAND B. - 26, Rue d'Étape
DUCHAUSSOY G - 9, Rue d'Étape
FEILLAULT J. - 33, Avenue Gambetta
HAUMARET J. - 1, Quai de l'Hôpital
PRÉVOST D. - 23, Quai du Général Leclerc

• PHARMACIES

GATEAU - 21, Rue Gabriel Cortel
LEMARQUAND - 14, Avenue Gambetta
MADELEINE (de la) - Centre Commercial de la Madeleine
MARCHÉ (du) - 14, Quai Ragobert
SAINT-ANDRÉ (de) - 64, Rue Jacques d'Auxerre

• MASSEURS - KINÉSITHÉRAPEUTES

BRANGER J.-P. - 47, Avenue Gambetta
DIGNAT B. - 6, Rue Davoust
MEDJIAN-PASCAL E. - 1, Rue Faubourg Saint-Jacques
POUX F. - 43, Avenue Roger Varrey

• INFIRMIÈRES

Mme **BOUGEROLLES** - Rue Bellevue
Mme **GRANDVAUX** - Boulevard Lefèvre-Devaux
Mme **MONNOIR** - Rue du Grand-Longueron
Mme **PERRIN** - Rue Marcel Aymé
Mme **SCHINDLER** - 16, Rue Guy Herbin

1. On a mal aux dents.

   C. Morange   F. Poux   J. Haumaret

2. On a mal aux yeux.

   M. Rossigneux   Gateau   H. Vouters

3. On a mal au cœur.

   E. Medjian-Pascal   M. Bolusset   J. Feillault

4. On a mal au ventre.

   N. Jeandot   J.-P. Branger   B. Bigand

5. On a mal à la jambe.

   G. Duchaussoy   F. Poux   D. Rouat

6. On a mal à la tête.

   Lemarquand   J.-M. Allemand   M. Bolusset

7. On a mal à la gorge.

   E. Medjian-Pascal   M.-A. Corbin   D. Carré

13

Draw a line to connect each health concern in Column A with the most logical advice to treat it in Column B.

A	**B**
1. Je suis en mauvaise forme.	a. Il faut rester au lit.
2. J'ai des frissons.	b. Il faut mettre un pull.
3. J'ai mauvaise mine.	c. Il faut faire du sport.
4. J'ai la grippe.	d. Il faut téléphoner au médecin.
5. J'ai mal aux dents.	e. Il faut prendre ta température.
6. Je suis fatigué(e).	f. Il faut prendre rendez-vous avec le dentiste.
7. J'ai de la fièvre.	g. Il faut dormir.

14 | A.

Organize the following list of body parts according to how many of them human beings have.

yeux / oreilles / nez / bouche / dents / figure / dos / tête / épaules / bras / ventre / gorge / mains / doigts / genoux / jambes / pieds / doigts de pied / cou / cœur

On a un(e):	On a deux:	On a beaucoup de (d'):
_____	_____	_____
_____	_____	_____
_____	_____	_____
_____	_____	_____
_____	_____	_____
_____	_____	_____
_____	_____	_____

B. Use the following information to draw a monster. First, read the sentences below and decide if each one is logical or illogical. If a sentence is logical, draw the body part or parts listed in the "Logical" column. If a sentence is illogical, draw the body part or parts listed in the "Illogical" column. For example, the first sentence is illogical; therefore, your drawing of the monster should start with **une tête**, from the "Illogical" column.

		Logical	**Illogical**
1.	Le genou est sur la tête.	trois têtes	une tête
2.	On a un œil.	deux cous	un cou
3.	On a dix doigts de pied.	un grand ventre	un petit ventre
4.	Il ne neige jamais en hiver.	trois oreilles	deux oreilles
5.	Quand on est en bonne forme, on a bonne mine.	quatre bras	trois bras
6.	On écoute avec le nez.	trois mains	quatre mains
7.	On étudie après une interro.	trois jambes	une jambe
8.	On va au cours à minuit.	trois pieds	un pied
9.	On peut skier à Chamonix.	sept doigts de pied	cinq doigts de pied
10.	Il n'y a plus d'eau au café.	deux cœurs	trois cœurs
11.	On ne peut pas porter de baskets à l'école.	un chapeau dans la main	un chapeau sur la tête

		Logical	**Illogical**
12.	On porte un chapeau sur la tête.	deux nez	un nez
13.	On a deux oreilles.	une grande bouche	une petite bouche
14.	On achète des fauteuils au supermarché.	trois dents	cinq dents
15.	On téléphone au médecin quand on a de la fièvre.	trois yeux	deux yeux

4) Rester dans cette position 3 à 4 minutes et revenir en déroulant tout doucement la colonne vertébrale (déconseillé en cas de lordose, scoliose, décalcification de la colonne vertébrale).

4. How long should you stay in this position?

_____

_____

5. Who should not do this exercise?

_____

_____

19 | Read the magazine article that follows. Begin by looking at the illustration and predicting what the article is about. After you have read it, answer the questions.

JOGGING : FAITES UN PARCOURS SANS FAUTES

TÊTE
droite, muscles du visage décontractés.

ÉPAULES
souples ; les bras, pliés à la hauteur de la taille, se balancent d'avant en arrière.

JAMBES
avec le genou légèrement fléchi quand le pied entre en contact avec le sol.

MAINS
avec les doigts repliés de façon naturelle.

TRONC
droit, légèrement penché vers l'avant.

PIEDS
qui prennent contact avec le sol par le talon et se déroulent. Terminez le mouvement par une poussée de l'avant-pied et des orteils.

Le jogging revient en force. Pratiqué 20 minutes trois fois par semaine, il maintient en parfaite condition physique. Cependant, il doit être pratiqué en respectant quelques règles.

UN ENTRAÎNEMENT PROGRESSIF ET RÉGULIER : si vous êtes débutante, les premiers jours, alternez une minute de jogging avec une minute de marche ; au bout d'une semaine, deux minutes de jogging avec une minute de marche. À ce rythme, vous pourrez courir vingt minutes d'affilée sans effort à la dixième semaine.

DES CHAUSSURES ADAPTÉES : achetez une paire de chaussures confortables, spécial jogging, adaptées à votre morphologie. La semelle, suffisamment épaisse, doit amortir les chocs de l'impact du pied. N'attendez pas qu'elles soient trop usées pour les remplacer.

UN TERRAIN SOUPLE : si le jogging peut se pratiquer n'importe où, privilégiez les chemins, les pistes de terre battue, les pelouses... aux surfaces lisses et peu dures. Si vous courez sur une route légèrement bombée, changez régulièrement de côté pour éviter que ce soit toujours le même pied qui entre en contact avec le niveau le plus élevé du sol.

---

1. What is the purpose of this article?

_____

2. According to this article, how often should you jog?

_____

3. For how long should you jog?

_____

4. If you are a beginner, what should you do during the first week of jogging?

_____

_____

5. What kind of shoes should you wear?

_____

Unité 11　*En vacances*

1 Identify the nationalities of the following people according to where they live.

　Modèle:　Rachel est de Rôme.
　　　　　　Elle est italienne.

1. Paul est de Madrid.

　　_____

2. Anne et Virginie, vous êtes de Luxembourg.

　　_____

3. Les Tourdot sont de Marseille.

　　_____

4. Madeleine est de Genève.

　　_____

5. Pierre et Victor sont de Boston.

　　_____

6. Élise, tu es de Québec.

　　_____

7. Laurent est de Bruxelles.

　　_____

8. Nancy et Chloé sont de Berlin.

　　_____

9. Je suis de Londres.

　　_____

2 Choose the best answer to each question according to the **Enquête culturelle** in **Leçon A**.

1. Whose memory do the French honor during the first two days of November?

　　_____ a. war veterans

　　_____ b. relatives and friends

　　_____ c. both a and b

2. What flowers are usually placed on graves during the November holidays?

_____ a. roses

_____ b. carnations

_____ c. chrysanthemums

3. Why is the French rail system so highly regarded?

_____ a. The trains are punctual.

_____ b. Gourmet food is served on all trains.

_____ c. The trains travel at 258 m.p.h.

4. What is the abbreviation for France's modern, fast train?

_____ a. SNCF

_____ b. HLM

_____ c. TGV

5. Who are the Walloons?

_____ a. Belgians who speak French

_____ b. Belgians who speak Dutch

_____ c. members of Napoléon's army

6. Which of the following foods is not a specialty of Belgium?

_____ a. gaufres

_____ b. frites

_____ c. pizza

7. What city is the capital of Belgium?

_____ a. Waterloo

_____ b. Brussels

_____ c. Paris

8. Which organization has its headquarters in Belgium?

_____ a. NATO

_____ b. the United Nations

_____ c. the Red Cross

3 | Read the sentences that follow. Indicate whether each one refers to the past, the present or the future by putting a check in the appropriate column.

	Past	Present	Future
Modèle: Je suis allé à Lyon hier.	✔		
1. Didier est à Paris.			
2. Tu vas rester au Canada.			
3. M. Mégy, vous n'êtes pas allé à l'école.			
4. Grégoire et Martin vont au centre commercial.			
5. Rosa vient d'Italie.			
6. Anne et Véronique sont restées avec Madeleine.			
7. Marc et Maurice vont arriver à huit heures.			
8. Tu es arrivée hier soir.			
9. Jean est parti avec sa mère.			
10. Élodie va rentrer après le film.			
11. Gérard est sorti avec ses cousins.			
12. Ma famille et moi, nous allons être en vacances.			

4 | **A.**   Rewrite the following paragraph, changing the infinitives to the **passé composé**. Be sure to make any necessary agreement between the subject and the past participle.

Patrick (sortir) avec Anna. Ils (partir) à sept heures. Ils (aller) au café, puis, ils (aller) au cinéma. Après le film, ils (rentrer) chez Anna. Patrick (arriver) à sa maison à minuit.

_____

_____

_____

_____

_____

Leçon B

7 | Identify the nationalities of the following people according to the country they are from.

Modèle: Suzette vient du Sénégal. *Elle est sénégalaise.*

1. Malick vient de République Démocratique du Congo. _____

2. Béatrice et Valérie viennent du Maroc. _____

3. Jamila vient de Côte-d'Ivoire. _____

4. Paul et Léonard viennent de Tunisie. _____

5. Véronique vient d'Algérie. _____

8 | Answer the following questions according to the **Enquête culturelle** in **Leçon B**.

1. What are the two international airports that serve Paris?

_____

_____

2. How did the Ivory Coast get its name?

_____

_____

3. What is the largest city in the Ivory Coast?

_____

4. What country is among the richest and most progressive in West Africa?

_____

_____

5. What is the relationship like between Senegal and France today?

_____

6. How does the Senegalese landscape vary?

_____

_____

7. What language do most Senegalese use at home?

_____

8. What is the capital of Senegal?

_____

9 Referring to the picture, match each person described in Column A with his or her position in line in Column B. Write the correct letter in the blank next to each number in Column A. The man with the dog is first.

	A		B
_____	1. un homme d'affaires	a.	premier
_____	2. un homme avec des fleurs	b.	deuxième
_____	3. une fille qui aime le camping	c.	troisième
_____	4. un garçon qui fait du roller	d.	quatrième
_____	5. une élève	e.	cinquième
_____	6. une femme avec un chapeau	f.	sixième
_____	7. un homme avec un chien	g.	septième
_____	8. une femme avec du pain	h.	huitième
_____	9. une mère avec ses enfants	i.	neuvième
_____	10. un vieil homme	j.	dixième

10 Using ordinal numbers, identify the sequential position on the calendar of the following months of the year.

Modèle: août *Août est le huitième mois.*

1. avril _____

2. mars _____

3. juin _____

4. février _____

5. septembre _____

6. novembre _____

7. mai _____

8. octobre _____

9. décembre _____

10. juillet _____

11. janvier _____

11 In which country do you find the following cities?

Modèle: Où est Paris? *Paris est en France.*

1. Où est Genève? _____

2. Où est Bruxelles? _____

3. Où est Londres? _____

4. Où est Madrid? _____

5. Où est Marseille? _____

6. Où est Québec? _____

7. Où est Abidjan? _____

8. Où est Dakar? _____

9. Où est Atlanta? _____

10. Où est Hô Chi Minh-Ville? _____

11. Où est Tokyo? _____

12. Où est Berlin? _____

13. Où est Rome? _____

14. Où est Bei-jing? _____

15. Où est Veracruz? _____

16. Où est Rabat? _____

12 Organize the following place names by writing each one in the appropriate column in the chart.

Saint Louis / Pierre / French Polynesia / Martinique / Madagascar / France / New Caledonia / Ivory Coast / Democratic Republic of the Congo / Senegal / Guadeloupe / Réunion / Des Moines / French Guiana / Haiti / Belgium / Luxembourg / Boise / Vietnam / Cambodia / Switzerland / Laos / Monaco

U.S. Cities with French Names	French Overseas Territories	French Overseas Departments	French-speaking Areas in Europe	Former French Colonies

15

Write the name of the place where you would go to find what is in each picture.

Modèle: *la gare* _____

1. _____

2. _____

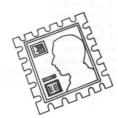

3. _____

4. _____

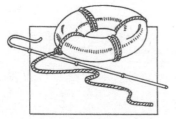

5. _____

6. _____

7. _____

8. _____

9. _____

10. _____

11. _____

16 | Answer the following questions according to the **Enquête culturelle** in **Leçon C**.

1. What is the capital of Luxembourg?

_____

_____

2. Where is the Camargue located?

_____

_____

_____

3. For what two animals is the Camargue famous?

_____

_____

4. How did Les Saintes-Maries-de-la-Mer get its name?

_____

_____

_____

_____

5. How are streets often named in France?

_____

_____

6. Where can you change money in France?

_____

_____

7. What are three things you can do at a French post office, other than buy stamps?

_____

_____

_____

8. Other than at a post office, where can you buy stamps in France?

_____

_____

17 Write a logical sentence using a subject from Column A, the corresponding present tense form of the verb **voir**, any item from Column B and its likely location from Column C. The first one has been done for you.

	A	B	C
1.	On	des assiettes	à la boutique
2.	Tu	des œufs	à la plage
3.	Ève et Lucie	des chaussures	à la poste
4.	Je	des timbres	au cinéma
5.	Patrick et moi, nous	des livres	au restaurant
6.	Delphine	des avions	à la bibliothèque
7.	Grégoire	des trains	à la gare
8.	Abdou et Karim	des films	à l'aéroport
9.	Solange et toi, vous	des maillots de bain	au marché

1. *On voit des timbres à la poste.* _____

2. _____

3. _____

4. _____

5. _____

6. _____

7. _____

8. _____

9. _____

18 | Read the travel article that follows. First, skim the article to determine its context. Try to form mental pictures as you read. Identify cognates to make sense of the article as a whole, and try to think in French as you read it. Finally, answer the questions that follow the article.

Au Maroc 359,00€

À l'Eldorador Palmariva, situé au cœur de la palmeraie de Marrakech, rien ne manque pour passer des vacances toniques. Entre la piscine, le tennis, la gymnastique, le golf, et les balades en VTT ou en moto 4 roues, le choix des activités est vaste. Sans oublier la visite des souks de la ville pour s'imprégner de l'atmosphère et des parfums orientaux. Au marché des fruits secs et des épices, on fait griller amandes et pois chiches. Un peu plus loin, les vanniers s'activent autour d'une montagne de corbeilles et de paniers. Et juste à côté, au souk des bijoutiers, on peut dénicher des trouvailles, en marchandant un peu. À faire absolument : une promenade sur les remparts et dans les parcs qui entourent la ville. Le soir, on apprécie la chambre spacieuse de l'hôtel qui donne sur de superbes jardins fleuris. Et on se laisse tenter par un tajine ou un couscous accompagné d'un vin du pays ou encore du fameux thé à la menthe, très désaltérant.

LE PRIX COMPREND le transport aérien, sept nuits en demi-pension, certaines activités sportives et les animations pour les enfants.

CLIMAT La température moyenne est de 18° C.

DÉCALAGE HORAIRE Une heure de moins qu'en France.

---

1. What is the purpose of this article?

    _____

    _____

    _____

2. Who might read it?

    _____

    _____

    _____

3. Imagine an illustration for this travel article. Based on your own experiences, what might it include?

    _____

    _____

    _____

4. What are at least five cognates in the article?

_____

_____

_____

5. What might interest someone in this trip to Morocco?

_____

_____

_____

6. What is the price of the trip and what does it include?

_____

_____

_____

7. What activities are available in Morocco?

_____

_____

_____

8. The first sentence says that nothing is missing for a healthy vacation. Why could this statement be considered an opinion?

_____

_____

_____

9. What is the climate of Morocco?

_____

_____

_____

Unité 12   *À Paris*

Leçon A

1 Read the list of buildings, monuments and other sights in Paris. Then, using the diagram, list buildings in the circle on the left and list monuments in the circle on the right. List monuments that are also buildings in the area where the two circles intersect. Finally, list the things that are neither monuments nor buildings outside the circles.

l'hôtel / le Louvre / le bateau / la Seine / la petite statue de la Liberté / Notre-Dame / le guichet / le tombeau de Jim Morrison / le métro / la tour Eiffel / le Drugstore / les jardins des Tuileries / l'arc de triomphe / le cimetière du Père-Lachaise

Buildings   **Monuments**

Both

Neither

2 Put a check next to the best answer to each question according to the **Enquête culturelle** in **Leçon A**.

1. What is the capital of French Polynesia?

    _____ a. Paris

    _____ b. Tahiti

    _____ c. Papeete

2. What is Tahiti's major industry?

    _____ a. hydroelectric power

    _____ b. tourism

    _____ c. landscape paintings

3. What is **le Drugstore**?

    _____ a. a café

    _____ b. a cemetery

    _____ c. a department store

4. Who painted *la Joconde*?

    _____ a. Leonardo da Vinci

    _____ b. François I

    _____ c. Frédéric Chopin

5. What is **un carnet**?

    _____ a. the subway system in Paris

    _____ b. a station where you transfer from one line to another

    _____ c. ten subway tickets

6. How do you refer to a Parisian subway line?

    _____ a. by number

    _____ b. by the stations at its end points

    _____ c. by color

7. Who is buried in Père-Lachaise cemetery in Paris?

    _____ a. Jim Morrison

    _____ b. François I

    _____ c. Leonardo da Vinci

8. What American monument has a small replica in Paris?

_____ a. the Washington Monument

_____ b. the Statue of Liberty

_____ c. the Liberty Bell

---

3 | Read the following statements about what two different people named Claude did while they were in Paris. One Claude is a woman; the other is a man. If you determine that a statement refers to the woman named Claude, put a check in the column labeled "Claude (f.)." If the statement refers to the man named Claude, put a check in the column labeled "Claude (m.)." If you can't determine which Claude the statement refers to, put a check in the column labeled "Claude (?)."

	Claude (f.)	Claude (m.)	Claude (?)
Modèle: Claude a marché sur les Champs-Élysées.			✔
1. Claude a quitté la gare du Nord à sept heures.			
2. Claude a mangé un croissant au café près de la gare.			
3. Claude est allé au marché.			
4. Claude a acheté des livres.			
5. Claude a décidé de prendre le métro à la tour Eiffel.			
6. Claude a regardé la ville du troisième étage.			
7. Claude est allée aux grands magasins.			
8. Claude est sorti des Galeries Lafayette à midi.			
9. Claude est entré dans un restaurant pour le déjeuner.			
10. Claude est restée au restaurant jusqu'à treize heures.			

4 **A.** Read the postcard that follows and circle all the verbs in the **passé composé**. If the helping verb is **être**, write the infinitive of the verb in the **Être** column. If the helping verb is **avoir**, write the infinitive of the verb in the **Avoir** column.

> Je suis arrivée à Paris ce matin. D'abord,
> je suis allée à la tour Eiffel. J'ai regardé
> la ville du 3ème étage. Puis, j'ai mangé au
> café près de Notre-Dame. Alors,
> j'ai décidé d'entrer dans cette église.
> J'ai acheté des fleurs au marché.
> J'ai continué mon chemin près de la
> Seine jusqu'au Louvre. Puis, je suis rentrée
> à l'hôtel.
> Grosses bises,
>   Suzanne

Michelle Jackson
42 Main St.
Smithville, PA
          08720

Être   Avoir

_____   _____

_____   _____

_____   _____

_____   _____

B. Now rewrite the message in the postcard from Part A to show how it would change if it were written jointly by Suzanne and her sister, Françoise.

> Nous sommes arrivées à Paris ce matin.
>
> _____
>
> _____
>
> _____
>
> _____
>
> _____
>
> _____
>
> _____

5 Tell what certain people did yesterday. Use a subject and the appropriate past tense form of a verb in Column A and complete the sentence with a logical choice in Column B. Use each item only once.

A	**B**
1. Marie-France / porter	a. un plan de métro
2. Sylvie et toi, vous / décider de	b. mon vélo
3. Luc et moi, nous / attendre	c. l'hôtel à sept heures
4. Tu / quitter	d. ses chèques de voyage
5. Thérèse / demander	e. nos amis à la gare
6. M. Bois / perdre	f. des baskets
7. Patrick et Sophie / manger	g. voir *la Joconde*
8. Je / vendre	h. des croissants au café

1. _____

2. _____

3. _____

4. _____

5. _____

6. _____

7. _____

8. _____

10 | Identify each of the following famous landmarks of Paris.

Modèle: *Notre-Dame* _____

1. _____

2. _____

3. _____

4. _____

5. _____

6. _____

7. _____

8. _____

11 Match each item in Column A with its description in Column B. Write the letter of your choice in the blank next to each number.

A

_____ 1. île de la Cité

_____ 2. Conciergerie

_____ 3. les bouquinistes

_____ 4. jardins des Tuileries

_____ 5. Parisii

_____ 6. la Ville lumière

_____ 7. île Saint-Louis

_____ 8. Pont-Neuf

_____ 9. Montmartre

_____ 10. place Charles-de-Gaulle

B

a. a small, residential island in the Seine

b. a Gallic tribe that settled what is now Paris

c. the oldest of more than 30 bridges across the Seine

d. the square in which the **arc de triomphe** is located

e. an artistic quarter of the city

f. the island where the city's history began

g. a nickname of Paris

h. a state prison during the French Revolution

i. the former gardens of French royalty

j. booksellers along the banks of the Seine

Leçon C

12   You have just returned from a vacation in Paris and you have been asked to write a short report about your trip. Use the following questions to write your report.

1. Comment est-ce que tu as trouvé Paris?

2. Qu'est-ce qu'on peut faire à Paris?

3. Quels quartiers sont les plus modernes?

4. Quels sont deux jolis jardins à Paris?

5. Est-ce que le Forum des Halles est à Paris?

6. Quelle est la plus belle ville du monde?

_____

_____

_____

_____

_____

_____

_____

13   If you were in Paris, where would you go to . . .

1. watch university students relaxing outside? _____

_____

2. try out a scientific experiment? _____

_____

3. shop at a large underground mall? _____

_____

4. see artists at work? _____

_____

5. see movies on a gigantic screen? _____

_____

6. go for a walk in the woods? _____

_____

14 | Using the map of the **arrondissements** of Paris and the information provided, determine whether these sights are on the left bank (**la rive gauche**—south of the Seine) or the right bank (**la rive droite**—north of the Seine). Write your answer on the line next to each item.

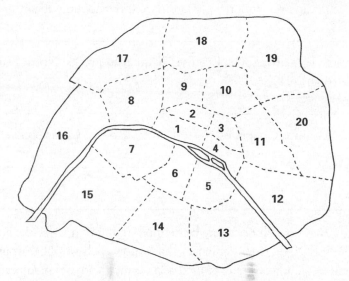

Modèle: les Invalides–septième arrondissement *la rive gauche*

1. les Champs-Élysées–huitième arrondissement _____

2. le jardin du Luxembourg–sixième arrondissement _____

3. les jardins des Tuileries–premier arrondissement _____

4. le Louvre–premier arrondissement _____

5. le Centre Pompidou–quatrième arrondissement _____

6. la tour Eiffel–septième arrondissement _____

7. le musée Picasso–troisième arrondissement _____

8. l'Opéra–neuvième arrondissement _____

15 | For each item, an adjective is followed by three choices, all within a certain category (in parentheses). Decide which choice the adjective best describes. Then write a sentence about your choice, using the superlative form of the adjective. Watch out for agreement!

Modèles: grand: la tour Eiffel / l'arc de triomphe / le Louvre (monument)

     La tour Eiffel est le plus grand monument.

     cher: le billet de cinéma / le billet d'avion / le billet de métro (billet)

     Le billet d'avion est le billet le plus cher.

1. vieux: le pont de Grenelle / le Pont-Neuf / le pont Alexandre-III (pont)

_____

2. moche: le tableau de Monet / le tableau de mon professeur / le tableau de Picasso (tableau)

_____

3. joli: les jardins des Tuileries / le jardin du Luxembourg / le jardin chez moi (jardin)

_____

4. moderne: le quartier de la Défense / le quartier près de Notre-Dame / le quartier du Louvre (quartier)

_____

5. blanc: la Sainte-Chapelle / Notre-Dame / le Sacré-Cœur (église)

_____

16 | French words, like English ones, can be defined in different ways, depending on the context in which they're used. The three sentences that follow each word below use the word in a different context. The word may be used as a noun, a verb or an adjective. Match the word with the best definition and write the letter of your choice in the blank next to the sentence. The first one is done for you.

1. **boîte** (n. f.)

    ___*c*___ J'ai une *boîte* de petits pois.   a. mailbox

    _____ Je vais en *boîte* ce soir.   b. dance club

    _____ Où est la *boîte* aux lettres?   c. can

2. **fondu** (n. m.), **fondue** (n. f.), **fondre** (v.)

    _____ J'aime le *fondu* de ce tableau.   a. to melt

    _____ J'ai mangé une *fondue* au restaurant.   b. blend (of colors)

    _____ Il a fait chaud et la glace a *fondu*.   c. specialty dish from Switzerland

3. **cuisine** (n. f.), **cuisiner** (v.)

    _____ Le four est dans la *cuisine*.   a. style of cooking

    _____ On a mangé de la *cuisine* française.   b. kitchen

    _____ Elle *cuisine* souvent pour ses amis.   c. to cook

4. **donné** (adj.), **donner** (v.)

    _____ J'ai *donné* des fleurs à ma mère.   a. fixed

    _____ La date est *donnée*.   b. to produce

    _____ Ce jardin *donne* beaucoup de fleurs.   c. to give